ENDORSEMENTS FOR
THE POWER OF TRUTH IN PERILOUS TIMES

The Power of Truth in Perilous Times was a surprising and delightful read. Most books I've read that purpose to draw distinctions between the spiritual decline in culture and the glorious riches found in Christ do so in ways that elevate the challenges and power of culture. Dr. Drake has done just the opposite. He has certainly detailed cultural challenges, but to a much greater degree, he has declared with great clarity that the God of the Bible does not bend a knee to contemporary culture, nor does he quiver in fear of the challenges culture can present. My heart was encouraged, and my faith strengthened. Dr. Drake frames every point biblically and wraps his points with practical illustrations and historical examples that make the book readable, understandable, and most importantly, livable. Every believer who struggles to be hopeful and live victoriously in the face of all the opposition the world presents us needs to read this book. Doing so will bolster a renewed spirit of faith in our Heavenly Father to do everything his Word says he will do and that he will be for us everything his Word declares him to be. Absolute truth has as its foundation the presence and power of God. Therefore, its truthfulness is eternal. It is true in every culture, for all times, and every person whose life has been transformed through the power of his gospel can build their lives upon it and live with joy and purpose in anticipation of Jesus' imminent return.

Dr. Charles Fowler
President
Carson-Newman University
Jefferson City, Tennessee

Marc Drake has written an important treatise for our times! Our culture is increasingly hostile to the Christian worldview and the concept of truth. Dr. Drake has presented a thoughtful and well-researched defense of both the existence and character of God as revealed in Scripture. This lays a solid foundation for knowing God and living out the truth. The book also includes appendices for the inevitable spiritual warfare a person will face and helpful resources for the battle. I highly recommend this book to counter the confusion we encounter in our country today.

Dr. David W. Johnson
Executive Director
Arizona Mission Network of Southern Baptists
Phoenix, Arizona

Dr. Marc Drake has brought multiple decades of pastoral experience and wisdom to offer much-needed clarity on pursuing God in the midst of the culturally chaotic moment. In a time when confusion, contradictions, and controversy muddy the waters through all the voices demanding attention, Dr. Drake gently, humbly, and winsomely reminds us of what is most important. Knowing, loving, and pursuing God is the first and most essential calling we are to pursue. In *The Power of Truth in Perilous Times*, Dr. Drake has written a very accessible, informative, and thoughtful book desperately needed today. I highly recommend this book and would encourage pastors, Christians, and seekers to read it.

Dr. Alan Bandy
Professor of New Testament and Greek
Robert L. Hamblin Chair of New Testament Exposition
New Orleans Baptist Theological Seminary

First, let me say, "God's timing" couldn't have been better when I began reading *The Power of Truth in Perilous Times*. You see, I was diagnosed with cancer not too long ago, and I found that Marc's book became a part of my daily devotional. The chapters on the attributes and promises of God were just what I needed.

The more I read through all the many people mentioned in the book, including Bible scholars and others, the more I realized that the great doctrinal truths of Scripture should cause us to bow in worship and wonder before the God of whom those doctrines are certainly true.

Larry Rea
Legends of the Outdoors Hall of Fame
Radio personality and motivational speaker
Memphis, Tennessee

Our world has lost its mind. The moral absurdity that swims in the wake of a few centuries of "enlightened" secular humanism is surely approaching its limit and bringing us to the verge of self-destruction. Is it time to "call it a day?" Is it time for the sane to give up and admit that our cultural moment has passed the point of no return? Or worse, is it time to fret and cower in the face of all the insanity? *The Power of Truth in Perilous Times* answers those questions with a definitive *no*. God is on his throne with no intention of abdicating. In fact, God is actively building his church, and the gates of hell will not prevail against it. In his book, Dr. Marcus E. Drake takes the reader on a journey from panic to praise by demonstrating that the road to sanity lies in knowing the God of the Bible, and the path to peace lies not in fearing the world but in fearing the One who created and sustains the world. Sprinkled with a heavy dose of hymns, practical application, and doctrinal groundwork, Dr. Drake's book reads much like an epistle from the apostle Paul—orthodoxy that leads to orthopraxy and ends in doxology. Yes, the world is full of sin. The culture is deteriorating. But God is bigger than sinful culture. He will win. And if we are his, we will be victors with him. It is no time to panic or fret or quit. Ours is a time to trust and pray and rest, which is to say: Ours is a time to worship the trustworthy God of Scripture. To that end and with the skill of a seasoned pastor, Dr. Drake lifts our hearts and minds to God and bids us sing the song of the redeemed in a strange and foreign land.

Eugene Oldham
Associate Pastor of Worship and Christian Education
Composer and choral arranger
Grace Church, Harrisburg, North Carolina

THE POWER OF TRUTH IN PERILOUS TIMES

Pursuing the Knowledge of God in the Midst of Cultural Insanity

Marcus E. Drake

ISBN 979-8-89309-277-6 (Paperback)
ISBN 979-8-89309-278-3 (Digital)

Unless otherwise indicated, all scripture quotations are from the ESV Bible (the Holy Bible, English Standard Version), copyright 2001 by Crossway, a publishing ministry of Good News Publishers. Used by permission. All rights reserved. Scripture quotations marked CSB have been taken from the Christian Standard Bible, copyright 2017 by Holman Bible Publishers. Used by permission. Christian Standard Bible and CSB are federally registered trademarks of Holman Bible Publishers. Scripture quotations marked NKJV are taken from the Holy Bible, New King James Version, copyright 1982 by Thomas Nelson, Inc. All rights reserved. Scripture quotations marked NASB are taken from the New American Standard Bible, copyright 1960, 1962, 1963, 1968, 1971, 1972, 1973, 1975, 1977, 1995 by the Lockman Foundation. Used by permission.

Covenant Books
11661 Hwy 707
Murrells Inlet, SC 29576
www.covenantbooks.com

To Pamela
A woman who *fears the Lord* (Proverbs 31:30), lives up to the
meaning of her name (sweeter than honey), and is the love of my life

To our grandchildren
Tennessee, Sawyer, Noah, Savannah, and Elliot
and their parents
Matthew and Natalie Drake
Joseph and Corrie Gallaher

Great is the Lord, and greatly to be praised,
and his greatness is unsearchable.
One generation shall commend your
works to another, and shall
declare your mighty acts. (Psalm 145:3–4)

In memory of Olan Hendrix,
a dear friend and mentor, who was a source of
constant encouragement to me as his pastor
and who urged me to write

O God, you are my God;
earnestly I seek you;
my soul thirsts for you;
my flesh faints for you,
as in a dry and weary land
where there is no water.

—Psalm 63:1

CONTENTS

FOREWORD

"What is *truth*?"

This question has been asked directly and indirectly by individuals for many generations. One notable person was a Roman governor in Judaea, who asked this question as he interrogated a "man" accused of serious crimes by a group of people. The Roman official was Pontius Pilate and the accused person was Jesus Christ, the Son of God. We don't know for sure the tone of Pontius Pilate's voice as he asked this question. And there isn't any indication that he waited for a reply.

More important than just seeking to understand Pontius Pilate's mindset during his encounter with Jesus is to consider the clear statement of Jesus Christ, the Son of God, that led to this question, "What is *truth*?" Pilate was interrogating Jesus among other things to find out what kind of king Jesus claimed to be. Jesus made it clear that his kingdom was "not of this world."

When Pilate went on to probe this matter of kingship, Jesus said, "You say that I am a king. For this purpose I was born and for this purpose I have come into the world—to bear witness to the truth. Everyone who is of the truth listens to my voice" (John 18:37).

Jesus Christ reveals to Pilate that the reason for his incarnation and ministry was that he might be king and testify to the truth. In this statement, Jesus is not only affirming that there is truth, but he is also stating that his purpose is to proclaim truth. He is a witness to the truth. Implicit also in his answer to Pilate is the identity of his followers that they are those who are "of the truth"; hence, they listen to his voice. What amazing claims, especially when you realize the context in which Jesus was speaking!

Jesus Christ, the Son of God, bore witness to truth. Indeed, he was and is truth (John 14:6). His people must necessarily be truth believers. Not long before this encounter with Pontius Pilate, Jesus prayed for his disciples. And he prayed that they would be sanctified "in the truth," stating also categorically in prayer to his Father, "Your word is truth" (John 17:17). Here we hear the Living Word, indeed the living truth, affirming the truth of the Word of his Heavenly Father. God's Word is *truth*.

God's Word is truth—this is the affirmation of Dr. Marc Drake in the volume in your hands. Furthermore, Dr. Drake affirms the truth of God's Word in the light of a present-day culture that challenges the very notion of absolute truth. Indeed, *truth* has fallen on hard times in our day. Rather than just cursing the darkness, Dr. Drake proclaims and explains glorious God-centered truth and truths that are the antidote for the waywardness and the *insanity* of the perilous times in which we live.

Many hearing Jesus Christ's claims concerning truth (presented above) may not respond any better than Pilate did. They may ask the same question as Pilate, but like Pilate, they may not take time to inquire further concerning this critical subject. There is a sense in which those who do not respond in faith and obedience to the truth of Jesus Christ will probably "give in" to the crowd and will allow Jesus to be crucified rather than crowned.

Dr. Drake helps us with "the right response" in *The Power of Truth in Perilous Times*. After he provides evidence for the very existence of God and the authority of his Word, Dr. Drake then focuses on understanding the character of God. Knowing God's attributes and his promises is a means to personal stability and spiritual growth. There is a danger in our day of seeking quick fixes and practical self-driven steps to face the challenges of the day. Any practical steps, though, must be based on solid truth and truths that lead to the renewing of our minds and indeed our hearts. Then whatever practical steps are taken will be based on the Word of God and the work of the Spirit of God. So we need to grow in our knowledge of God himself as he has revealed himself to us in his Word, the Scriptures.

The purposeful challenge of this book is expressed in the subtitle, *Pursuing the Knowledge of God in the Midst of Cultural Insanity*. Dr. Drake focuses on two very important biblical doctrines to help us grow in the knowledge of God. He explains what it truly means to fear the Lord and to bear his image. Such truths should be viewed in contrast to the self-centered strategies for life and living that need to be cast aside. Pursuing God and the knowledge of God are to be our priorities.

The supreme importance of this pursuit is underlined by another statement by our Lord Jesus in the prayer found in John's Gospel, chapter 17. As he prayed, Jesus defined eternal life in this way: "This is eternal life, that they may know you the only true God, and Jesus Christ whom you have sent" (John 17:3). True knowledge of God and indeed of Jesus himself are the essence of eternal life. Indeed, eternal life can be expressed as the experience of truly knowing God and his Son. Eternal life is a gift of God, and so is the privilege of knowing God. What a blessing to be able to grow in that knowledge of God and his Word.

Dr. Drake is helping us grow in that knowledge. Then he provides a fitting conclusion and very helpful appendices to end this book. I encourage the reader to benefit from appendix 1 as we are led in appropriate prayers based on the armor of God. The reader will find great encouragement also in the many insights that Dr. Drake gives us throughout this volume. The reader will be blessed by numerous helpful quotations, including the poetic words of powerful hymns, many of which have stood the test of time.

Recently, I talked with someone who is very concerned about Christians taking a stand in these perilous days. This is what Dr. Drake is doing in this book. Because he is not dabbling in fringe issues nor seeking some "new revelation," some may not be interested. But solid truths for life and living come from the Word of God. There is no substitute for the truth of the Word of God. God's Word is our authority, and God's Word is sufficient for all matters of faith and practice for life and godliness. This is true in our day as it always has been true.

Jesus' people are people "of the truth." Also, they are people who hear his voice above the many alternative messages of our day. We need to be people "of the truth," for the truth, and living by the truth. Biblically and pastorally, Dr. Drake both challenges us and comforts us with the powerful truths of God's Word. If the reader will take to heart what is presented in this volume, a serious response will lead to greater stability by God's grace in these perilous times. And stability is what is needed as we seek to be faithful servants of the Lord and faithful witnesses to the truth in our day.

Many years ago, when Dr. Drake lived in the Memphis area, we got to know his passion for the Lord and his Word. It is no surprise that his passion has continued and is now expressed in this helpful book. This book is a testimony to the power of the truths of God's Word to save, strengthen, and sustain us as is evidenced in the life and ministry of its author.

David L. Olford
President, The Stephen Olford Center for Biblical Preaching
Olford Ministries International
Memphis, Tennessee

ACKNOWLEDGMENTS

Thank you to Dr. David Olford who graciously consented to write the foreword to this book and whose meaningful words scripturally frame the theme of the book. For many years, the Stephen Olford Center for Biblical Preaching, where David serves as president, has brought rich and rewarding personal growth and biblical teaching to my life; for this, I am deeply grateful. I also rejoice in the highly significant impact of Olford Ministries International throughout the world.

Gratitude is expressed to Brian Eckley, my group leader for the Colson Fellows program—a training ministry of the Colson Center for Christian Worldview. It was while I was involved in my teaching project (for which Brian gave oversight) that the idea for this book first began to take root in my thinking.

I also want to express my heartfelt gratitude to those who took the time to review my manuscript and to give their kind, written endorsements. I am humbled and honored by your words, and I treasure your friendship.

Furthermore, a special word of gratitude goes to my wife, Pamela; son, Matthew; and friends Larry Rea, Joe Tatum, and Eugene Oldham for blessing me with their expertise—whether in proofreading, technical help, suggestions, advice, encouragement, or prayer support. You have made a difference!

Also, I express my thanks to George and Joan Shuttleworth, diligent students of the Word, faithful prayer partners, and gracious encouragers to my wife and me.

Soli Deo Gloria!

INTRODUCTION

What God Is Doing

In today's confused culture, many people can probably identify with Christopher Columbus who didn't know where he was going when he started, didn't know where he was when he got there, and didn't know where he had been when he got back! Of course, God knew. He also knows where *we* are, where we have been, and where we are going in terms of his sovereign plans for our lives and ministries in the midst of a chaotic world.

We cannot change the culture but God can. At the same time, he uses his people to lovingly yet boldly proclaim the gospel of the kingdom of God to their communities and to the nations. It all begins by acknowledging his adequacy and our inadequacy. As it has often been said: he's God...we're not!

Therefore, the purpose of this book is to show how the knowledge of God, as defined and described in the Bible, impacts our own lives and then the lives of others as God works through us in the midst of a culture that has utterly lost its way. Thus, I am not writing to simply decry the devastating changes in our nation and world but rather to proclaim the unshakable hope that is ours in the very nature and character of God himself, the identity and security we have in Christ, and the guidance we need in order to be salt and light in our generation.

This is not to say, of course, that everyone will respond to the truth once they hear it or even that most people will respond, but God can soften and open hearts, and he has promised that his Word "shall not return to me empty, but it shall accomplish that which I purpose, and shall succeed in the thing for which I sent it" (Isaiah 55:11).

Therefore, God's children must fervently and consistently ask him to implant his Word deeply in them (Psalm 25:4–5), asking him for a renewed passion to read it, study it, and meditate on it. Evangelist and author Vance Havner noted that how long a person has been a Christian only tells how long he has been on the road. It doesn't tell how far he has come.

So to go far spiritually, one must go deep biblically. Determine then that you will pursue the knowledge of God by immersing yourself in his Word every day (2 Timothy 2:15). The result will be a greater love for the one who created and redeemed you, more consistency in applying his Word to life, and daily transformation through the power of the Holy Spirit. Out of this kind of renewal will come the authority to communicate the truth to others with accuracy, clarity, authority, and joy—all for God's glory alone.

Moreover, it is important to recognize at the outset that the knowledge of God is the basis for our entire lives, and it gives us the foundational principles for how we are to live in this world. Thus, understanding what this scriptural concept means is extremely important. Proverbs 2 teaches us that if we seek godly wisdom, we "will understand the fear of the Lord and find the knowledge of God" (Proverbs 2:5).

Therefore, the more we know God (his nature and his ways) and are devoted to him, the more we will live out his purposes each day and the greater will be our effectiveness in proclaiming the truth of his Word. Certainly, if ever there was a time to lovingly yet boldly confront our culture with the knowledge of God, it is today!

Of course, this will not be popular with many people. Christian apologist Brett Kunkle has written:

> In our lifetimes, we have never seen the pressure on Christian conviction greater than it is right now. We try to avoid alarmism, but standing for Christ in our culture is getting harder and harder.[1]

Pastor John MacArthur goes so far as to say that our culture has reached the bottom of the diabolical spiral described in Romans 1:21–32. He has written:

> People not only commit and heartily approve gross evil; they demand everyone's participation in the public celebration of wickedness.[2]

The apostle Paul spoke of such people, calling them "enemies of the cross of Christ" and saying that they "glory in their shame" (Philippians 3:18–19).

So how do we live and minister in such a society? How do we respond to the moral morass and cultural insanity of our day? Many people wonder why God would allow these kinds of things to happen. The better line of thinking, however, is to focus on the actual work God is doing in our culture and world today and ask him to show us how we can align ourselves with his purposes. In actuality, God is doing what he has always done, as J. I. Packer summarizes beautifully:

> What is God doing? He is "bringing many sons unto glory" (Heb. 2:10). He is saving a great company of sinners. He has been engaged in this task since history began. He spent many centuries preparing a people and a setting of world history for the coming of his Son. Then he sent his Son into the world in order that there might be a gospel, and now he sends his gospel through the world in order that there may be a church. He has exalted his Son to the throne of the universe, and Christ from his throne now invites sinners to himself, keeps them, leads them, and finally brings them to be with him in his glory.[3]

May we never lose sight of this glorious perspective of God's ongoing work in our world—that of saving sinners through the atoning blood and bodily resurrection of his ascended, exalted, and eternally reigning Son!

Therefore, as we think about the mighty work God is doing in the world and the extraordinary impact biblical truth can have on our culture, we will focus on three vital and foundational areas in Scripture: how God reveals his existence through nature and his Word, how God discloses his character through his attributes and promises, and how God calls his people to seek the knowledge of himself through the fear of the Lord and the bearing of his image.

Although there are a number of issues that come to mind when we think about the culture war in our nation, Charles Colson identified the heart of the matter:

> The real war is a cosmic struggle between worldviews—between the Christian worldview and the various secular and spiritual worldviews arrayed against it. This is what we must understand if we are going to be effective both in evangelizing our world today and in transforming it to reflect the wisdom of the Creator.[4]

Since a view of origins (the beginning of the physical world) is an important part of any worldview, it is necessary to begin by examining the evidence for the existence of God and his supernatural work as the Creator. As Colson has stated: "Creation is the first element of the Christian worldview, the foundation on which everything else is built."[5] Therefore, when confronted with the question of whether the universe is governed by random material forces or by an intelligent, sovereign Creator who is personal and loving, it is crucial that we are able to accurately explain the clear evidence for the latter.

Thus, in the midst of our confused and deteriorating culture, believers are called to live as Christ followers who cherish the truth, understand and live out a biblical worldview, and constantly pursue the knowledge of God as presented in Scripture. These are vitally important concepts that we will explore in the coming pages.

Read on...

PART 1

Weighing the Evidence
Exploring the Existence of God

CHAPTER 1

Seeing...but *Not* Seeing

On August 7, 1961, a twenty-six-year-old Russian became the second Soviet cosmonaut to orbit the earth and return safely. Sometime later, he was speaking at the World's Fair, and as he recounted his experience in space, he let it be known that he had not seen God up there. Dr. W. A. Criswell, then pastor of First Baptist Church of Dallas, replied forthrightly: "Let him take off his space suit for just one second and he'll see God quick enough."[1]

A few years later, on Christmas Day of 1968, three American astronauts were the first humans to go around the so-called dark side of the moon, away from the earth. Once they were bound for home on Apollo 8, they beheld our planet in a way human eyes had never seen before.

They saw the earth covered in a beautiful mixture of white and blue as it rose over the horizon of the moon and bordered by the glimmering light of the sun against the blackness of space. In the midst of this awe-inspiring experience, these American astronauts opened the pages of the Bible and read for all the world to hear, "In the beginning, God created the heavens and the earth" (Genesis 1:1).

Obviously, the Russian cosmonaut and the American astronauts had two very different conclusions about the nature of the world. In fact, they carried into space the most debated question on earth: Does God exist? In other words, has God created man or has man created God?

There are people today who are not convinced of the existence of God. What do we say to them? Actually, there may not be much we can say to those who (for whatever reason) reject outright the evidence for God's existence. No amount of evidence can make them believe in God if they do not *want* to believe in him.

However, for those who are intellectually honest and will give us a hearing, we could begin by pointing out that "every effect must have a cause equal to or greater than itself."[2] There must be something or someone—in existence uncaused—from which everything else in existence has derived.

Therefore, the best explanation for the origin of all things is a divine Creator. As William Lane Craig has stated, "Amazing as it may seem, the most plausible answer to the question of why something exists rather than nothing is that God exists."[3] In other words, if he didn't create the universe, what other option is there? It would be quite nonsensical to suggest that the universe made itself; how could a universe that didn't exist have the power to do *anything*, let alone create itself? The obvious reality is that we live in a universe that is filled with order, intelligence, and design—all of which points to a divine designer, God himself (facts we will presently consider more fully).

Perhaps in talking with someone about spiritual matters, you have faced the question: But how can I know there is a God? To answer this question, you must point to the evidence for his existence. If you just say, "Well, I know he's real because I can feel him in my soul" (as an old song suggested), then the skeptic may say, "Good for you, but that's not my experience. I don't feel him, so maybe he's not real after all."

As believers, we certainly do have a wonderful sense of God's presence in our lives, but God is not real because I can feel him. For example, what if I wake up one morning and I don't feel him within me like I did the day before? Does that mean that God is no longer real—that he died during the night? Of course not.

Therefore, let's focus on the explicit evidence that God himself has given us for his existence—evidence that is based on reality and has nothing to do with feelings. The truth is that God has chosen to reveal himself in two ways: through *nature* and through his *Word*. Thus, in this chapter, we will take a look at the evidence for God revealing himself through nature as seen in Romans 1:19–20.

The Universal Revelation of God

The context in verses 18–20 is that of ungodly people who suppress the truth, which means they are attempting to stifle or obscure it in order to get it out of their minds. The reason they cannot do so is because, as the apostle Paul says, "For what can be known about God is *plain* to them, because God has shown it to them" (Romans 1:19, emphasis mine). So try as they might, they cannot eradicate the truth of God's existence because he keeps declaring it through what he has created!

Thus, Paul is teaching that through the creation, all people everywhere have the opportunity to recognize and know the reality of God's existence—all people...everywhere!

God has indeed revealed himself *universally*.

Winston Churchill said to the House of Commons on May 17, 1916, "The truth is incontrovertible. Panic may resent it, ignorance may deride it, malice may distort it, but there it is."[4]

Likewise, the truth of God's existence is unmistakable. *There it is!* The Creator has displayed his abilities and power in such a way that no one can rightfully say, "I never knew there was a God." This is why Paul says at the end of verse 20 in Romans 1 that "they are without excuse"—an expression that means "without defense."

Thus, in his treatment of this verse, Professor Ralph Earle has written: "Those who close their eyes to the revelation of God in nature will have no defense in the day of judgment. How much more those who refuse to read or follow God's written Revelation, the Bible!"[5]

Yet there are those who do not accept God's revelation of himself in nature, much less his revelation in Scripture. Many of them claim that all of what we *are* and *have* is simply because of random chance. They claim they don't believe in God; they are atheists. But God is saying in essence (based on Romans 1), "I don't believe in atheists." The reason for this is because *he* knows that *they* know (deep down inside) that there is a Creator! After all, it should be obvious that such unique design and beauty could never come about by accident or random chance.

Scientist Jonathan Wells has stated, "When you analyze all of the most current affirmative evidence from cosmology, physics, astronomy, biology, and so forth…the positive case for an intelligent designer becomes absolutely compelling."[6]

So it appears that professing atheists are trying to persuade themselves to *disbelieve* something—something that is inescapably inscribed on their hearts—and that's the fact that there is a God and they are accountable to him. The Greek term for *plain* in verse 19 clearly indicates that the knowledge God reveals about himself is not obscure. It is plain, visible, clear, known… It is there for all to see.

Thus, while many people continue to reject God's universal revelation of himself, it is still there. In fact, Ecclesiastes 3:11 says that God has put *eternity* in man's heart. This is why there has never been a tribe of people discovered anywhere on earth—no matter how small or how savage—that has not believed in some kind of god or had some form of worship. New Testament scholar Jeremiah Johnston affirms this reality:

> Archaeological work everywhere, in every corner of the world, finds temples in every ancient city. In fact, one can safely say that there was no city or civilization in human history that did not have at least one temple or building whose primary purpose was a religious one.[7]

Moreover, missionaries have discovered that people groups throughout the earth who have had no access to the teaching of Scripture still know that they have sinned. Thus, when a Christian comes to them and talks about sin, he often finds that they readily admit this to be true. Such a reality points to the clear evidence of God's existence, as well as man's sin *against* him and his need *for* him.

The Natural Revelation of God

Let's go further with how God has revealed himself in nature. Through the design, exactness, precision, and beauty of creation, he has clearly and spectacularly pointed to himself as the Creator. Hence, those with eyes to see recognize the truth of Psalm 19:1, "The heavens declare the glory of God, and the sky above proclaims his handiwork."

Likewise, Romans 1:20 says, "For his invisible attributes, namely, his eternal power and divine nature, have been clearly perceived, ever since the creation of the world, *in the things that have been made.* So they are without excuse" (emphasis mine).

Yes, it is clear that what God has made testifies eloquently to his existence. Just as an artist reveals himself in what he draws or paints or sculpts, so the divine Artist has revealed himself in creation. In amazing ways, his majesty and power are stamped on what he has made, thus displaying his invisible attributes through his visible creation.

The English Puritan Thomas Brooks said, "What are the heavens, the earth, the sea, but a sheet of royal paper, written all over with the wisdom and power of God?"[8] So when we consider the incalculable vastness and amazing design of the universe, it is abundantly clear that God is communicating to humans his existence and power.

During the days of the French Revolution, one of the revolutionaries boasted to a peasant, "We're going to pull down all that reminds you of God."

The peasant replied, "Pull down the stars then!" Precisely. That peasant obviously understood Psalm 19:1—that the *heavens* declare the glory of God himself. The amazing design and celestial precision of the universe are simply undeniable!

Therefore, through what he has made, the God who is unknowable has made himself knowable (albeit not as fully as he has in his Word, as we will explore in chapter 2). Creation then points to the existence of God and to the fact that he is a transcendent, intelligent, powerful, personal, and moral being—a reality that Paul is clearly teaching in Romans 1:20. Thus, there is nothing irrational about believing in the existence of God.

Yet many people still hold to the idea that there was some kind of random cosmic explosion back in the eons of time that resulted in a perfectly designed, well-ordered universe—a universe that is, in fact, far more complex in its design and function than anything humans could ever produce. Moreover, a big bang back in the cosmic past would not have resulted in order; it would have resulted in disorder. That's the nature of explosions!

It has been reported that Roger Penrose, who helped to develop black hole theories, estimated that the odds of a big bang producing by accident an orderly universe as opposed to chaos are one in one hundred billion to the 123rd power![9] How does one even begin to comprehend such odds?

At its heart then, evolution is believing that an explosion of nothing, initiated by no one, accidentally brought about everything! Or to put it succinctly, *nothing times nobody equals everything.* How could any equation possibly be more preposterous?

So what *did* bring the universe into existence? Why is there something and not nothing? Did it all just come about by chance as many believe? The truth, however, is that chance has no power to do anything. Why? Because chance is *not* anything; it has no being and, therefore, does not exist. So how can something that is nothing do anything? In fact, it's not even something if it is nothing!

As theologian R. C. Sproul has said in his inimitable way:

> What are the chances that chance can do anything? Not a chance. It has no more chance to do something than nothing has to do something.[10]

He's absolutely right. For example, if your bank account has zero balance, it would be unreasonable to check the statement every month to see if you've earned interest. Nothing is nothing and never becomes something!

But it *is* reasonable to say that someone—that is, the eternal God himself—brought the universe into existence from nonexistence. In other words, he alone brought something out of nothing because he existed *before* there was anything.

In no uncertain terms, the Bible declares, "In the beginning, God created the heavens and the earth" (Genesis 1:1). As a result, we can categorically say that before there was anything, there was God. He is eternal and uncreated.

Therefore, since God existed before creation, he had to create the universe (and everything in it) out of nothing—that is to say, without the use of any previously existing materials. As Romans 4:17 declares, God "gives life to the dead and calls into existence the things that do not exist." Who but God could do that?

In summary, we can see clearly that the beauty, order, and cosmic precision of the universe had nothing to do with random chance but rather testifies to the existence and power of God alone as the Creator. Thus, when we look at creation, we are beholding clear proof that behind all its intricate design, there is a divine designer. The heavens indeed are declaring the glory of God and his handiwork.

Therefore, it is very important to take the time to peer into the vast depths of sky and space to behold the work of our glorious, all-powerful Creator. We don't have to be an astronaut (or even buy a telescope) to see the glory of God in what he has created. All we have to do is look up!

Furthermore, consider the human body with its remarkable design and function. Theologian Paul Enns, for example, points out that the eardrums are recessed sufficiently to prevent children from poking their fingers into their ears and damaging them. He also notes that if our nostrils were turned upward, we could drown in a rainstorm![11] Yes, without a doubt, the human body is the production of a Master Creator.

Moreover, many scientists have come to realize that life—even at the level of a single cell—is much too complex to have evolved. For example, we are told that the average human body is comprised of thirty trillion cells and that the genetic information contained in each of these cells is roughly equivalent to a library of four thousand volumes. Imagine: thirty trillion cells in one body, and each of those cells has that much genetic information! No wonder the more that scientists discover about the astonishing design of the human body, the less credibility there is for evolution.

Life in a fallen world does not evolve from the simple to the complex or from disorder to order. Would a person ever deduce that a computer suddenly happened upon out in a desert had merely evolved into its present state over millions of years? What about the carvings on Mount Rushmore? Who would look at those four faces and surmise that they came about over long periods of time as nothing more than the result of wind, rain, and glacial erosion with no human design and careful workmanship involved?

Similarly, British astronomer Sir Frederick Hoyle stated, "The chance that higher life forms arose by evolutionary processes is comparable with the chance that a tornado sweeping through a junkyard might assemble a Boeing 747 from the materials therein."[12]

Therefore, if things on earth clearly reflect a human designer, how much more should the universe reflect a *divine* designer! It makes much more sense to discard evolution and believe instead—as Paul declared in his sermon on Mars Hill—that God "gives to all mankind life and breath and everything. And he made from one man every nation of mankind to live on all the face of the earth" (Acts 17:25–26).

Yes, God is the One who made us—and all thirty trillion cells in us. Thus, the evidence for the existence of God is based on creation itself. Therefore, when all things are considered, there is nothing unreasonable about believing in the existence of God. We have unmistakable evidence.

The Continual Revelation of God

Furthermore, Paul teaches in Romans 1:20 that "since the creation of the world," God's invisible attributes have been clearly perceived through the things he has made. Thus, God is *constantly* declaring his incomparable glory, greatness, majesty, and power through his creation.

Paul's words in verse 20 confirm the witness of King David hundreds of years earlier when, after speaking of the heavens declaring the glory of God, David goes on to say in Psalm 19:2, "Day to day pours out speech, and night to night reveals knowledge." That is to say, the constant communication of the heavens is proclaiming the existence and nature of Almighty God.

Thus, having looked at the clear and continual evidence God plainly displays in order to reveal his eternal power and divine nature (Romans 1:20), we must now ask: Why then have multitudes come to deny or question a Creator and believe instead that humans just evolved from lower life-forms? Why are students regularly taught in public schools and universities that their lives are simply the result of a cosmic accident with life having emerged through nothing more than the chance collision of atoms and moving inexorably toward the abyss of nothingness at the end? A concept that will certainly not put joy in the heart or spring in the step!

Perhaps the answer to why people cling to evolution and secular humanism is because such a worldview puts man at the center of everything and removes any kind of divine authority and moral accountability. Therefore, if this life is all there is and ultimately leads to nothing, should we not go after all the pleasure we can find regardless of how it might affect other people?

John Lennon of the Beatles imagined no heaven or hell and people simply living for today.

However, is "living for today" while recognizing no accountability to a Creator truly meeting the basic needs of human beings? It certainly offers no meaningful answer to life's questions such as: Where did I come from? Why am I here? Where am I going? Does life have any purpose?

Not surprisingly, as John Stonestreet has pointed out, "Despair is taking hold at a time when we have almost unlimited access to fun, pleasure, and distraction."[13] He goes on to quote from *The Everlasting Man* by G. K. Chesterton:

> Pessimism is not in being tired of evil but in
> being tired of good. Despair does not lie in being

weary of suffering, but in being weary of joy. It is
when for some reason or other the good things in
a society no longer work that the society begins
to decline; when its food does not feed, when its
cures do not cure, when its blessings refuse to
bless.[14]

Ironically, while humanists and evolutionists tell us that our
existence starts and ends in meaninglessness, they hastily declare at
the same time that we are creatures of great dignity. Do they not
recognize the muddled thinking reflected in such a conclusion? If,
after all, I am nothing more than a grown-up germ on the way to
nothingness, I will sense no purpose in life whatsoever—let alone
great dignity! I'm reminded of a quip from humorist Woody Allen:

More than any other time in history, mankind faces a crossroads. One path leads to despair
and utter hopelessness. The other, to total extinc-
tion. Let us pray we have the wisdom to choose
correctly.[15]

Thankfully, there is another option! It is the Christian worldview—the polar opposite of secular, humanistic thinking and the
only one that provides believers with unshakable hope, irrepressible
joy, and the indisputable knowledge that, come what may, their lives
are in the hands of God (and there is no better place to be).

Thus, the contrast could not be greater. On the one hand, the
secular worldview considers the human race as nothing more than
the result of a cosmic accident that happened eons ago, as well as
involving millions of years of evolution. Not surprisingly, this worldview (which clearly lacks credible evidence) allows for no other option
for explaining life on this planet—much less life after death. On the
other hand, the Christian worldview reveals joyous biblical hope in
the solid, undeniable evidence that we are individuals who have come
into being by the direct creative act of an intelligent, eternal being.

Sadly, however, many people still reject the truth about God and turn away from him. This is why Paul says in Romans 1:21, "For although they knew God, they did not honor him as God or give thanks to him, but they became futile in their thinking, and their foolish hearts were darkened." Then in verse 25, he writes, "They exchanged the truth about God for a lie and worshiped and served the creature rather than the Creator, who is blessed forever!" What a sad commentary these verses give us concerning an individual or a society that rejects the truth and embraces deception and idolatry. "To reject God, the Father of truth, is to become vulnerable to Satan, the father of lies" (John 8:44).[16]

Moreover, as G. K. Chesterton has pointed out, when we reject the God of the Bible, we don't believe in nothing; we believe in everything.[17] Thus, to seek spiritual satisfaction outside of God and his Word is to be void of discernment altogether and to enter the wide gate and easy way "that leads to destruction" (Matthew 7:13).

The former president of the Czech Republic Václav Havel once expressed grave concern over the moral condition of his country. In describing the culture of lies that had engulfed communist Czechoslovakia, he said this:

> Because the regime is captive to its own lies, it must falsify everything. It falsifies the past, it falsifies the present, and it falsifies the future. It falsifies statistics. It pretends not to possess an omnipotent and unprincipled police apparatus. It pretends to respect human rights. It pretends to persecute no one. It pretends to fear nothing. It pretends to pretend nothing.[18]

These words speak powerfully to the deception, corruption, and rejection of truth in our own society today. Evidence abounds that we live in a day when people have rejected the truth of God for a lie. One could point to Marxist ideology, critical race theory, transgenderism, and the proabortion industry—all of which are undeniably anti-God and exalt arrogant, humanistic thinking. Eric Metaxas points to the emergence of such ideas and forces, writing with a much-needed warning:

> It's easy to see this with regard to Germany in the 1930s, when we think of the death camps and the murder of so many millions, but we need to understand that in the beginning they had no idea where it was leading, and had no idea they were facing nothing less than the forces of anti-Christ. We are now facing those same forces in different guises.[19]

Of course, the rebellion of man changes nothing when it comes to the nature of God. As C. S. Lewis put it, "A man can no more diminish God's glory by refusing to worship him than a lunatic can put out the sun by scribbling the word 'darkness' on the walls of his cell."[20] Thus, God goes right on revealing evidence for his existence and work.

Clearly then, when people sincerely examine the evidence about God, they must conclude that there is nothing unreasonable about believing in his existence. For example, if we believe that a complex set of instructions—such as we have in DNA—needs a designer and a blueprint requires an engineer and a moral law requires a moral lawgiver, then surely it is much more so a sign of intelligence and rationality to believe in the reality of God himself.

Indeed, the evidence for the existence of God is overwhelming. He reveals himself universally, naturally, and continually. However, he has revealed himself much more intimately than that which is observable in nature. The power of God, and to some extent his attributes, are seen in creation, but the *person* of God is revealed in his Word.

Yet how do we know the Scriptures are reliable and entirely true? This is the fascinating subject of the next chapter.

CHAPTER 2

Into the Courtroom

How would you respond if someone asked, "Why do you believe what you believe?" Hopefully, you wouldn't simply say, "Well, that's just what I have *always* believed" or "That's what I was *taught* to believe." Rather, you should heed the words of the apostle Peter when he instructs believers to "make a defense to anyone who asks you for the hope that is in you" (1 Peter 3:15).

The story is told of the famous evangelist George Whitefield, who asked a man what he believed. The man said, "I believe what my church believes."

Whitefield asked, "What does your church believe?"

The man said, "My church believes what I believe."

Then Whitefield asked, "Well, what do you both believe?"

The man said, "We both believe the same thing!"

I don't know if Whitefield ever got a straight answer out of him! Obviously, that man had nothing more than secondhand opinions, and those are certainly not a clear basis for one's beliefs. On the other hand, the Bible *does* provide a clear and true basis for what we believe; it is the very voice of God and, as such, is fully authoritative and completely sufficient in every way. For just as it is clear that God has revealed himself in nature (as we saw in chapter 1), it is also clear that he has revealed himself through his Word and through his Son, who *is* the Word (John 1:1).

The Bible says, "All flesh is like grass and all its glory like the flower of grass. The grass withers, and the flower falls, but the word of the Lord remains forever" (1 Peter 1:24–25).

Based on this passage, and many others as well, it is obvious that the Bible is truly God's eternal Word. John MacArthur has written:

> If there is one word that best describes the Christian worldview, it is truth. In an age of changing opinions, multiple perspectives, and varying viewpoints, biblical Christianity stands by itself as objective, absolute, and abiding truth. Scripture alone teaches us how to perceive the world in a way that accurately corresponds to reality. As such, its message of salvation is as timely as it is timeless. And its truth is as reliable as it is unchanging.[1]

Therefore, when someone says, "Why do you believe what you believe?" you can point them to the full authority of Scripture. Suppose, however, you are conversing with someone who says, "How do I know that the Bible is true and trustworthy? After all, it was written by humans, and humans make mistakes." How would you respond to the person?

Obviously, when questions about the Bible come up, it is important to address them. We must never get into an argument over the nature of Scripture, of course, but rather patiently show people the abundant evidence God has provided that his Word is inerrant and fully authoritative.

In fact, at this point, it is as though you have entered the courtroom and you are presenting undeniable evidence that the Bible is without error and, thus, perfectly reliable. In doing so, you're giving a defense of *what* you believe and *why* you believe it—a defense that is in line with 1 Peter 3:15.

So let's consider seven evidences that God's Word is completely true, fully authoritative, and all-sufficient.

Scientific Accuracy

The Bible, of course, is not a science textbook, but it is correct when it speaks on matters of science. The reason for this is that the same God who created what the scientists study also wrote the Scriptures.

Therefore, true science and the Bible are not in conflict, and science has never proved the Bible wrong. The fact is that science is an ongoing process of learning. This means, of course, that from time to time, the things once claimed to be true are later found to be false. Thus, the *latest* word in science is not necessarily the *last* word!

Clearly, this was understood by Joseph H. Taylor, an astrophysicist and Nobel laureate, who saw no conflict between science and theology. He said, "Our knowledge of God is made larger with every discovery we make about the world."[2]

However, others have discounted the reality of God such as Stephen Hawking, the brilliant physicist and mathematician at Cambridge University. He has been quoted as saying, "When I was younger, I wanted to know how and why the universe works. Now I know how, but I still don't know why."[3]

Hawking admitted that science, with all its strident gains, must still remain contented to describe the *what* of human observations but could not answer the *why*. The truth, of course, is that no amount of science can answer the *why* question—even simple questions like "How did everything begin?" and "What is the purpose of our existence?"

So, apparently, Stephen Hawking gave up asking the question *why* and became an atheist. He referred to heaven or the afterlife as "a fairy story for people afraid of the dark," to which Oxford professor John Lennox aptly responded, "And atheism is a fairy story for people afraid of the light."[4]

Exactly. And while nature itself provides a certain amount of light (as we saw in Romans 1), it is the Bible that gives us the much fuller revelation of God—his person and work. It is in Scripture that the *why* questions are answered (at least many of them). Thus, over

17

the centuries, scientific discoveries have only confirmed the reality of God, the universe he created, and the book he wrote!

For example, evolutionary English philosopher Herbert Spencer said that everything in the universe fits into five categories: time, force, action, space, and matter. No doubt many people at the time celebrated his brilliance. Yet, as John MacArthur has pointed out, Genesis 1:1 accounts for all of Spencer's categories: "In the beginning," that's *time*; "God," that's *force*; "created," that's *action*; "the heavens," that's *space*; and "and the earth," that's *matter*.[5]

There it is—all of it—in that first simple (yet wondrously profound) verse of the Bible. Thus, it seems that three thousand years later, science finally affirmed the very truth God has declared all along! In commenting on Spencer's categories, MacArthur goes on to say:

> In the first verse of the Bible God laid out plainly what no scientist or philosopher cataloged until the nineteenth century. Moreover, what evolution still cannot possibly explain— the actual origin of everything that science can observe—the Bible explains in a few succinct words in the very first verse of Genesis.[6]

Another example centers on the question that people have asked over the centuries: What holds up the world? As one might imagine, many strange and outlandish answers have been offered over the centuries, but the Bible answers the question in Job 26:7 by pointing to our Creator, saying, "He stretches out the north over the void and hangs the earth on *nothing*" (emphasis mine). Now if people had read and believed this many centuries ago, they would have known back then what science discovered only a few hundred years ago: the earth is suspended in space.

Furthermore, although we know the earth is round, for centuries, people thought it was flat; many believed that if you sailed far enough, you would go over the edge. However, some 750 years before Christ was born, Isaiah spoke of the greatness of God by saying, "It is he who sits above the circle of the earth" (Isaiah 40:22). The Hebrew word for *circle* does not indicate a flat disk. Rather, it means *globe, sphere*, or *ball*.

The people in Isaiah's day, of course, did not know the topography of the earth, but through divine inspiration, Isaiah declared that it was round! In fact, it was the Scriptures that inspired Christopher Columbus to sail *around* the world with the primary purpose of spreading the gospel—something we know because of the journal he left behind.

So how did Job know the earth is suspended in space? How did Isaiah know the earth is round 2,200 years before Columbus set sail? The answer is that God revealed it to them. Thus, it can be stated categorically that the Bible (God's written revelation) and true science are not in conflict with one another. Science only confirms the accuracy of the Bible.

The first piece of evidence then for the trustworthiness of Scripture is the scientific accuracy of the Bible, yet it is by no means the full extent of the evidence.

Historical Accuracy

Like scientific discoveries, historical ones have also repeatedly authenticated the statements of the Bible as entirely reliable. In fact, archaeology has "established the historicity of the people and events described in the Bible, yielding more than twenty-five thousand finds that either directly or indirectly relate to Scripture...the archaeological data we possess clearly indicates that the Bible is historically reliable and is not the product of myth, superstition, or embellishment."[7]

One of the world's foremost biblical archaeologist Nelson Glueck excavated over one thousand sites in the Middle East. After years of meticulous research, he said this: "It may be stated categorically that no archaeological discovery has ever controverted a biblical reference."[8] That is a powerful statement from a world-renowned archaeologist regarding the stunning evidence of Scripture's historical accuracy, especially when one considers that multiplied thousands of archaeological discoveries have taken place. Furthermore, places, people, and events have been carefully verified and chronicled through countless excavations.

For example, it used to be said that Moses could not have written the first five books of the Bible because writing was unknown at that time. Eventually, however, archaeologists unearthed tablets in Northern Egypt and found business transactions between people in Egypt and Palestine centuries before Moses was born! Thus, this gives perspective to what we are told in Acts 7:22, "And Moses was instructed in all the wisdom of the Egyptians."

Another example of archaeology confirming the biblical record is found in Daniel 5 where we read the story of Belshazzar, king of Babylon. However, secular history teaches that the king at that time was Nabonidus. Thus, critics of the Bible saw this as yet one more example of how Scripture contradicts itself. Eventually, however, a cylinder with an inscription on it was discovered in the Euphrates River, revealing that there were actually two kings of Babylon during a certain period of time, a father and a son. When he left to carry out military campaigns in Arabia, Nabonidus entrusted his son, Belshazzar, with the position of coregent.

Interestingly, this discovery throws light on Daniel 5:29 where we are told that Belshazzar appointed Daniel as the third ruler in the kingdom. Therefore, Daniel was the *third* ruler because there were already two others, Nabonidus and Belshazzar. Once again, archaeology validates the total trustworthiness of Scripture.

A final example of the Bible's historical accuracy is seen in a discovery regarding the Hittites who were a group of people mentioned numerous times in Scripture, yet until the nineteenth century, there was no archaeological evidence that this group ever existed—a reality that caused a number of scholars to suggest that the Bible was not historically accurate.

However, in the early twentieth century, a great number of artifacts were discovered that proved beyond any doubt that the Hittites had existed after all. In fact, included in the discovery were thousands of clay tablets, and once deciphered, they documented to the world that the lost Hittite Empire had been found—an empire that was centered in Turkey and extending into Syria.

Many other highly significant archaeological contributions have unquestionably substantiated the historical accuracy of the Bible. In speaking to Old Testament historical issues, archaeologist John Elder sums it up very well when he writes:

> Little by little, one city after another, one civilization after another, one culture after another, whose memories were enshrined only in the Bible, were restored to their proper places in ancient history by the studies of archaeologists... The overall result is indisputable. Forgotten cities have been found, the handiwork of vanished peoples has reappeared, contemporary records of biblical events have been unearthed and the uniqueness of biblical revelation has been emphasized by contrast and comparison to the newly understood religions of ancient peoples. Nowhere has archeological discovery refuted the Bible as history.[9]

Indeed, the spades of archeologists keep turning, and the evidence keeps mounting for the absolute truthfulness of God's Word.

Undeniable Unity

As we think about the unity of the Bible, consider these facts: the Scriptures were written in three languages (Hebrew, Greek, and a small portion in Aramaic) and that they were written by some forty human authors over a period of more than 1,500 years.

Furthermore, the Bible was written in countries far apart and even on different continents (Asia, Africa, and Europe). The biblical writers were from every walk of life—kings, generals, prime ministers, peasants, philosophers, poets, statesmen, fishermen, shepherds, and scholars.

Yet in light of such diversity, there are no contradictions or inconsistencies in Scripture but rather a profound unity throughout its pages. John Blanchard points to this remarkable fact when he writes:

> Although its writers deal with the most important questions that have ever occupied men's minds, and write on a great number of controversial subjects, they do so with a harmony and continuity that are unique in all literature.[10]

Furthermore, the indisputable unity of the Bible is seen in that it presents one glorious, unfolding theme from Genesis to Revelation. That theme, of course, is the story of God's plan of salvation for undeserving sinners—a story that centers on the person and work of Jesus Christ. Thus, the perfect unity of the Bible clearly reveals the mighty hand of God.

Therefore, as the result of divine authorship, all parts of Scripture fit together into a perfect whole. Thus, the unity of the Bible is a strong evidence for its complete trustworthiness.

But there's more...

Continual Translation and Circulation

The Bible has been read by more people and translated into more languages than any other book; it is never off the printing press. Billions of copies of the Scriptures have been disseminated. In fact, the Bible has been printed and distributed more than any other book in history and was even carried to the moon! It is far and away the best-selling book of all time. These facts also provide clear evidence for the divine authority of Scripture.

Furthermore, believers have boldly circulated the Bible among those who were forbidden to have it. On the contrary, have you ever heard of people trying to smuggle the writings of Shakespeare or Hans Christian Andersen into Saudi Arabia, China, or North Korea? Have you ever heard of anyone being jailed or executed for distributing copies of *Grimm's Fairy Tales*?

Yet the Bible—which some have called nothing more than a mere collection of myths—has been smuggled into places by people who risked their very lives to do so. This, too, is powerful evidence that the Bible is perfectly true and totally trustworthy.

Consider also the advances over the years in the translation process. Two hundred years ago, the Bible—or a part of it—was available in just sixty-eight languages. Today, the Bible has been translated into hundreds of languages and dialects while at least two thousand languages around the world are still awaiting a translation project to begin.

It is also instructive and fascinating to consider the fact that missionaries have gone to people groups with no written language, yet by living among the people, the missionaries have learned the significance of their words, built an alphabet and grammar, and then put the Bible into that language. As a result, multitudes throughout the world have come to faith in Christ.

God has promised to prosper his Word, and he has! He says in Isaiah 55:11, "So shall my word be that goes out from my mouth; it shall not return to me empty, but it shall accomplish that which I purpose, and shall succeed in the thing for which I sent it."

Thus, we must always remember this remarkable truth: God's Word never returns without accomplishing his sovereign purposes. Thank God for the continual translation and circulation of his living Word! A. Z. Conrad, a Boston pastor in the early twentieth century, said that the Bible "outlives, outlifts, outloves, outreaches, outranks, outruns all other books."[11]

Unique Survival

God's Word contains the oldest books in the world; the first portions were written over three thousand years ago. But through all those centuries, God has preserved his Word even though numerous and powerful people have tried to destroy it.

In fact, the Bible is the most persecuted book in all of history, having been attacked by emperors, popes, kings, and scholars. The Scriptures have been banned, burned, ridiculed, and outlawed.

Furthermore, entire Marxist regimes have launched massive attacks on the Bible, destroying millions of copies in every nation they controlled—all in a feverish effort to discredit and destroy the Scriptures. But these enemies of God's Word never succeed in their efforts.

For example, in AD 303, the Roman Emperor Diocletian fiercely opposed Christianity and tried to eradicate it, to the point where every family caught with a Bible was to be put to death. Bibles were confiscated and burned, and thousands of Christians were killed. This emperor actually thought he had brought an end to the Bible and to Christianity. He even erected a column inscribed with the Latin words *Extincto nomine Christianorum*, which means: "The name of the Christians has been extinguished."

But this emperor could not have been more wrong! Only ten years passed before Diocletian himself became "extincto" and a new emperor arose by the name of Constantine, who professed faith in Christ, ordered the writing of many copies of the Scriptures, and encouraged all the people in the Roman Empire to read the Bible.

Now this, of course, does not mean that all of them became true Christians, but you can see how quickly things can change. Man rises up in pomp and arrogance and declares himself a deity and attempts to decree Christianity extinct. However, as history has repeatedly shown, man does not have the last word.

For example, the famous agnostic Robert Ingersoll once made the statement that he would have the Bible in a morgue in fifteen years. Providentially, at the end of those years, Ingersoll was in a morgue and the Bible lives on!

Likewise, the story is often told of Voltaire, a well-known atheist, who dared to make the statement in 1788 that in a hundred years, there would not be a Bible. However, one hundred years later, Voltaire's house was owned and used by the Geneva Bible Society to spread Bibles all across Europe. I love the divine sense of humor in these accounts!

Consider the remarkable story of William Tyndale who was devoted to translating and publishing God's Word—even at the risk of his own life (which he subsequently lost as a martyr). On one occasion, a bishop became angry over the distribution of Bibles Tyndale had printed, and he sought to get them out of circulation. The bishop sent a friend to buy all of them in order that they might be destroyed. He instructed his friend, "Whatever it takes, buy them and destroy them."

The bishop's friend found Tyndale and purchased all his Bibles even though the price was exorbitant. The man then took those Bibles and destroyed them. However, with the money Tyndale had received from this sale, he bought materials to print thirty times as many Bibles and then had them distributed all over the country.

When the flustered bishop found out about this, he asked his friend where Tyndale had gotten the money to do this. The man said, "You paid for it—you bought the Bibles and he distributed them."[12]

Yes, many people have predicted the demise of the Bible and have sought to bury it. However, the "corpse" has outlived the pallbearers! And it always will. Why? Because the Bible is the living and eternal Word of God, having been *produced* by him and then *preserved* by him. If it had simply been the work of humans, it would have been destroyed long ago.

So who has the last word? Diocletian? Voltaire? Ingersoll? History answers with a resounding *no*! Neither does anyone else have the last word. Only God has it. He has supernaturally preserved the Scriptures, and he will continue to do so.

> The grass withers, and the flower falls, but the word of the Lord remains forever. (1 Peter 1:24–25)

Thus, the very survival of Scripture is further evidence of its divine inspiration, full authority, and complete trustworthiness. However, there is even more evidence that God's Word is completely true and all-sufficient.

Fulfilled Prophecies

Winston Churchill once quipped, "The main qualification for political office is the ability to foretell what is going to happen tomorrow, next week, next month, and next year—and to have the ability afterwards to explain why it didn't happen."[13]

The good news is that in his perfect wisdom and power, God never has to explain why something didn't happen that he said would happen. All his prophecies come true. Always!

Joshua declared to the people of Israel shortly before he died, "You know in your hearts and souls, all of you, that not one word has failed of all the good things that the Lord your God promised concerning you. All have come to pass for you; not one of them has failed" (Joshua 23:14).

Accordingly, it is highly significant that of the approximately 2,500 prophecies in the Bible—which comprises about 30 percent of Scripture—not a single prophecy has ever been shown to be false. Furthermore, about 2,000 of the total number of prophecies have already been perfectly fulfilled while the remaining 500 relate to end-time events yet to come. It is also important to realize that biblical prophecy is very specific unlike modern-day "prophets" who so often deal in generalities.

Consider, for example, the prophecies of Isaiah who ministered from about 740 BC and foretold numerous future events. Most notably, he declared in precise detail the coming of the Messiah (Isaiah 9:6–7), his virgin birth (Isaiah 7:14), his miracles (Isaiah 32:1–4), his rejection by the Jews (Isaiah 53:3), and his death by crucifixion (Isaiah 53:5, 12). Obviously, Isaiah did not make vague prophecies; rather he was very specific in his details. All that he had written came to pass several hundred years later exactly as he predicted.

The death of Jesus, the Messiah, was, of course, not the end of the story; he rose from the dead and, forty days later, ascended to heaven where he reigns eternally. These events were also predicted in the Old Testament hundreds of years before they occurred. Consider Psalm 16:10 and Psalm 68:18 for the resurrection and ascension of Jesus respectively. All in all, there are over three hundred prophecies in the Old Testament about the coming of Jesus Christ—prophecies that have already been perfectly fulfilled.

So how do we account for such complete accuracy regarding Old Testament prophecies about Christ? The answer is that the Bible ultimately has one author, the Holy Spirit. As 2 Peter 1:21 says, "For no prophecy was ever produced by the will of man, but men spoke from God as they were carried along by the Holy Spirit."

In addition to the specific Old Testament prophecies about Christ, there are many other prophecies that have been fulfilled to the letter. For example, there are predictions about specific kings (their rise and their downfall), the destruction of nations, the captivity of the Jewish people and then their release, and Israel's kingdom being restored. Obviously, the odds of specific and detailed prophecies being fulfilled just coincidentally are too enormous to be taken seriously.

Thus, fulfilled prophecy is one of the strongest arguments possible for the complete accuracy and total reliability of God's Word. Remember, if God wrote it, it has to be true. Moreover, Jesus himself acknowledged the full and unchangeable authority of the Bible, saying, "The Scripture cannot be broken" (John 10:35). Consequently, not a single biblical prophecy has ever been proven to be false.

Transforming Power

The Bible has not been given to us, as John Blanchard points out, "Merely for our information, but for our transformation, so that, as its message grips our minds and changes our hearts, we might have a God-centered worldview and lifestyle."[14]

The story is told of a woman who once called the Atlanta library and asked where Scarlett O'Hara was buried. The librarian told her that Scarlett O'Hara is a fictional character in Margaret Mitchell's novel *Gone with the Wind*. After hearing this, the caller said, "Never mind that. I want to know where she's buried." Apparently, the woman failed to grasp the meaning of the words *fictional* and *novel*! In her mind, Scarlett O'Hara was made alive in Mitchell's book.

Sometimes a person will say to a preacher or teacher, "You make the Bible come alive." The truth, however, is that the Bible is *already* alive. For unlike Scarlett O'Hara, the Bible is an eternal, living book (Hebrews 4:12). Furthermore, it's the book that makes *us* come alive (1 Peter 1:23)!

Just think of all the changed lives throughout history, and you quickly recognize the tremendous evidence that the Bible is true. For example, many years ago, a man by the name of A. W. Milne went to a part of New Guinea inhabited by cannibals. Not surprisingly, he encountered massive spiritual darkness in that area of the world. Yet through his faithful preaching, one after another of those fearsome cannibals became born-again servants of Jesus Christ. When Milne's ministry finally ended with his death, he was buried in the midst of the people he loved and led to Christ. They placed a marker on his grave with this inscription:

> Here lies the remains of A. W. Milne,
> When he came to us, there was no light,
> When he died, there was no darkness.

What a great epitaph for a man who invested his life in penetrating massive spiritual darkness and evil with the transforming light of the gospel! In his book *Loving God*, Charles Colson describes the dramatic power of God's Word to change lives and impact nations:

> Literary classics endure the centuries. Philosophers mold the thoughts of generations unborn. Modern media shape current culture. Yet nothing has affected the rise and fall of civilization, the character of cultures, the structure of governments, and the lives of the inhabitants of this planet as profoundly as the words of the Bible.[15]

Yes, over the centuries, countless lives have been transformed—from savages in remote regions of the world to white collar executives in corporate America. Pages of Scripture have been smuggled into prison cells, resulting in hardened criminals and killers being radically changed. Whole villages around the world have been brought to faith in Christ through hearing the living Word of God. It should be obvious that there can be no adequate explanation for these changed lives other than the fact that God has honored and used his Word as it has been proclaimed in the power of the Holy Spirit.

Social critic Dennis Prager has given us a good way to think about this. He was once debating the Oxford atheistic philosopher Jonathan Glover, and Prager had a question for him:

> If you, Professor Glover, were stranded at the midnight hour in a desolate Los Angeles street, and if, as you stepped out of your car with fear and trembling, you were suddenly to hear the weight of pounding footsteps behind you, and you saw ten burly young men who had just stepped out of a dwelling coming toward you, would it or would it not make a difference to you to know they were coming from a Bible study?[16]

Well, I think such news would even make an atheist feel better! Yes, it's true: God doesn't simply use the Bible to *inform* people; he uses it to *transform* them—something that has been happening for millennia.

This transformation, of course, comes about through knowing Jesus Christ personally for the forgiveness of our sins and the power of the Holy Spirit to live not for ourselves but for God and his glory.

Conversely, before coming to faith in Christ, we had no first-hand knowledge of him, no true love for him, and no regard for the sacredness of his name. But all is now profoundly different for those who are *in Christ*. His name has become the melody of our hymns, the basis of our prayers, the theme of our witness, and the strength of our life. Formerly, Jesus was nothing to us. Now, however, he is everything! He is our Savior, our Lord, our all in all.

> The old has passed away; behold, the new
> has come. (2 Corinthians 5:17)

This life-transforming power is clearly expressed through a delightful and well-known experience of the great twentieth-century preacher Harry Ironside. He was once challenged to a debate by an atheist who claimed that atheism had done more for the world than Christianity. Ironside accepted the challenge if his critic would agree to one condition: at the agreed upon hour for the debate, the atheist would have to bring with him at least two authentic witnesses who had been saved from lives of disgrace and degradation through their belief in atheism. Ironside, on the other hand, would have one hundred men and women with him who had been saved out of the darkness and despair of life and brought into the kingdom of God.

Not surprisingly, the atheist quickly retreated, and the debate never took place!

These seven evidences then show that God's Word is completely true, fully authoritative, and all-sufficient. Therefore, we can have full confidence in what the Bible says about itself and rejoice in the fact that all of Scripture is "breathed out by God" (2 Timothy 3:16). Thus, as Paul Enns has written: "Scripture is the product of the breath of God. The Scriptures are not something breathed into by God; rather, the Scriptures have been *breathed out* by God."[17]

Does this mean that the human writers were simply listening to a voice and writing mechanically every word? Was this simply dictation? No, the Scripture was flowing through their heart, soul, mind, emotions, and experiences. Yet due to the supernatural guidance of the Holy Spirit (2 Peter 1:21), every word came out as the very Word of God. Not surprisingly, no expert in any field or discipline has ever disproved a single statement in the Bible. Not one! Brian Edwards summarizes:

> The inspiration of Scripture is a harmony of the active mind of the writer and the sovereign direction of the Holy Spirit to produce God's inerrant and infallible word for the human race.[18]

Yes, all of Scripture is breathed out by God, as 2 Timothy 3:16 tells us. Furthermore, the latter part of the verse states that his Word is "profitable for teaching, for reproof, for correction, and for training in righteousness" (2 Timothy 3:16). Thus, J. C. Ryle (1816–1900) encourages us to remember the authority and power of God's Word to do its work in our lives:

> Do not think you are getting no good from the Bible, merely because you do not see that good day by day. The greatest effects are by no means those which make the most noise, and are most easily observed. The greatest effects are often silent, quiet, and hard to detect at the time they are being produced.
>
> Think of the influence of the moon upon the earth, and of the air upon the human lungs. Remember how silently the dew falls, and how imperceptibly the grass grows. There may be far more doing than you think in your soul by your Bible reading.[19]

Therefore, what could be of greater importance than knowing and believing God's perfect Word and applying it to our lives every day? It is living and active (Hebrews 4:12) and has the power to expose and convict, as well as to comfort, edify, and heal.

However, some professing Christians fail to grasp the necessity of truly basing their lives and ministries on God's Word. I once pastored a church where a man criticized the pastoral staff for using the Bible too much! I suppose that's kind of like criticizing a builder for using blueprints too much or a singer for using music too much or an artist for using paint too much.

Yet if I and other pastors have been criticized for using the Bible too much in our ministries, then we are in good company. The nineteenth-century preacher Charles Spurgeon was also criticized for his emphasis on Scripture. He decided to address the matter in a straightforward way. So one Sunday, when the time came for the reading of the Bible, he left it closed.

Spurgeon then explained, "Some have found fault with me, contending that I'm too old-fashioned. I am always quoting the Bible and do not say enough about science. Well, there's a poor widow here who has lost her only son. She wants to know if she will ever see him again. Let's turn to science for the answer: Will she see him? Where is he? Does death end all?" There was a long pause... "We are waiting for an answer," Spurgeon said. "This woman is anxious." Another long pause... Then Spurgeon called out, "Nothing to say? Then we'll turn to the book!" He then went on to read the promises of the Bible concerning heaven and eternal life.[20]

Undoubtedly, you have heard the statement countless times, "It all depends on how you look at it." Vance Havner has said, "Nothing depends on how we look at it... Everything depends on how *God* looks at it, and what He says about it in His Word."[21]

To hear it stated another way, an old Puritan preacher is reported to have commented, "There are two things I want to know. One, does God speak concerning the matter? And two, what does God say?"

Thomas Jefferson, however, was apparently not convinced that all of Scripture was the authoritative Word of God. It is well-known that he went through his New Testament with a pen and marked out all the references that offended him—that is to say, all the verses about God's wrath, hell, judgment, and so forth. Now it is hard to imagine a Bible-believing Christian being so brazen as Jefferson in actually deleting a part of God's Word. However, we may be guilty of a similar offense if we deliberately ignore any portion of what God has revealed to us in Scripture. If we accept the Bible as the perfect revelation of God and his will for our lives, then we can know that he has wasted no words in this Book.

All of them are important.

All of them are purposeful.

Consequently, we must read the Word, study the Word, and meditate on the Word. Moreover, it is on the basis of God's Word that we pray, praise, offer thanksgiving, and intercede for others—trusting the Holy Spirit for guidance through it all.

Furthermore, consider this: God reveals himself through his Word, and through his Word, he reveals himself in his Son. Hebrews 1:1–2 declares, "Long ago, at many times and in many ways, God spoke to our fathers by the prophets, but in these last days he has spoken to us by his Son."

Yes, God has revealed himself in Scripture, and he has primarily done it through his Son, the Lord Jesus Christ. To encounter Christ is to look into the very face and heart of God. Now while we can observe the majesty and power of God in creation, we know nothing of his personal love, mercy, and peace until we meet Jesus Christ. And it is throughout all of Scripture that we see him.

For example, consider the two disciples on the Emmaus Road in Luke 24. This was after the resurrection of Jesus, and they were walking along, talking about the crucifixion. Then suddenly, Jesus himself walked up and joined them although they didn't recognize him at first. The Bible says, "And beginning with Moses and all the Prophets, he interpreted to them *in all the Scriptures* the things concerning himself" (Luke 24:27, emphasis mine). Thus, Jesus was revealing himself through the teaching of the Old Testament.

Moreover, the Bible declares that Jesus came to reveal the Father (John 1:18). Thus, all Jesus is and does explains who God is and does; God the Son makes God the Father known. This is why Jesus said to Philip, "Whoever has seen me has seen the Father" (John 14:9). As a result, Jesus himself is the answer to the question, "What is God like?"

In teaching on both the divine and human nature of Christ, Ignatius of Antioch (AD 107) said this:

> There is one physician: He is both flesh and
> spirit; he is born and unborn; he is God in man;
> he is true life in death; he is from Mary and from
> God; he first suffered and then was beyond suf-
> fering; he is Jesus Christ our Lord.[22]

The coming of Jesus was planned in eternity past and prophesied throughout the centuries until in "the fullness of time" he appeared (Galatians 4:4). No greater gift has ever been given! As Carl F. H. Henry put it, "The early church didn't say, 'Look what the world is coming to.' They said, 'Look what has come into the world.'"

Thus, the redeemed can surely rejoice and confess with the apostle Paul as he exults:

> Blessed be the God and Father of our Lord Jesus Christ, who has blessed us in Christ with every spiritual blessing in the heavenly places, even as he chose us in him before the foundation of the world, that we should be holy and blameless before him. (Ephesians 1:3–4)

In answer to the question, "What evidence is there for the existence of God?" we can say that God has revealed himself through nature (creation), and he has revealed himself more fully through his Word (the Bible). Furthermore, through the Bible (his *written* Word), God has revealed himself in his Son (the *living* Word).

Thus, as we have seen, there is overwhelming evidence of the Bible's infallibility. In Psalm 19:7, David declares, "The law of the Lord is perfect." Therefore, in light of this truth, it stands to reason that the Bible must govern the way we think and live.

As you know, we live in a world where evil is called good and good is called evil. That which is right is now considered wrong, and that which is wrong is now declared right. It is crucial, therefore, that the Scriptures inform our thinking on the moral and ethical topics of the day such as abortion, infanticide, euthanasia, genetic engineering, same-sex marriage, cohabitation, and gender identity.

Obviously, we must know the Scriptures in order to understand what God says about these and other issues. The reality, of course, is that we live in a culture that often does the *opposite* of what the Bible teaches. However, if we have a biblical worldview, we will know how to think concerning the issues of our day and how to respond to the cultural insanity so evident in our nation. The following words from Robert Chapman bring solid instruction, much encouragement, and clearly reveal the authoritative nature of the Bible:

> This book contains the mind of God, the state of man, the way of salvation, the doom of

sinners, and the happiness of believers. Its doctrines are holy, its precepts binding, its histories are true and its decisions are immutable. Read it to be wise, believe it to be safe, and practice it to be holy. It contains light to direct you, food to support you, and comfort to cheer you. It is the traveler's map, the pilgrim's staff, the pilot's compass, the soldier's sword, and the Christian's charter. Here paradise is restored, heaven opened, and the gates of hell disclosed. Christ is its grand subject, our good its design, and the glory of God its end. It should fill the memory, test the heart, and guide the feet.

Read it slowly, frequently, prayerfully. It is a mine of wealth, a paradise of glory and a river of pleasure. It is given you in life, it will be opened at the judgment, and be remembered forever. It involves the highest responsibility, rewards the greatest labor and condemns all who will trifle with its sacred contents.[23]

Thus, in knowing the Scriptures, we are able to know God and better understand what he is actually like. This is the exciting subject of the next section.

PART 2

Glorious Attributes and
Powerful Promises
Understanding the Character of God

CHAPTER 3

Pondering the Imponderable (1)

Theologian R. C. Sproul was once asked, "What is the greatest need of people in the world?"

He answered, "People in the world need to know who God is."

Then Sproul was asked, "What is the greatest need of people in the church?"

He answered, "People in the church need to know who God is."[1] In profound simplicity, Sproul's answers spoke to the heart of the matter. For no matter who a person is, the greatest need in life is to know God as he is clearly presented on the pages of Scripture.

Therefore, as believers, our goal should be to continually grow in our understanding of God's majestic character. The great nineteenth-century preacher Charles Spurgeon put it like this:

> Nothing will so enlarge the intellect, nothing so magnify the whole soul of man, as a devout, earnest, continued investigation of the great subject of the Deity. Would you lose your sorrow? Would you drown your cares? Then go, plunge yourself in the Godhead's deepest sea; be lost in his immensity; and you shall come forth as from a couch of rest, refreshed and invigorated. I know nothing which can so comfort the soul; so calm the swelling billows of sorrow and grief; so speak

peace to the winds of trial, as a devout musing
upon the subject of the Godhead.[2]

In eloquent language, Spurgeon calls for us to think deeply about
God. To do so is to meditate on his Word by pondering his attributes
and rejoicing in his promises. This will lead us to wholeheartedly worship the one who is our Creator, Redeemer, and loving Shepherd.

Sadly, many people today do not have a biblical concept of God
at all, and, as we have seen, some will say that they do not even
believe in God. However, as is often the case, the God they don't
believe in does not actually exist, and this is because they have the
wrong concept of him. Therefore, we must ask them what they mean
by the terms they use; it could be something entirely different from
what the Bible teaches.

A. W. Tozer famously said, "What comes into our minds when we
think about God is the most important thing about us."[3] So if we are to
know and communicate the nature of God with biblical precision, we
must be ever pursuing the knowledge of God ourselves. "There never
has been an era when too many people thought too deeply about God or
knew him too well. It is impossible to know God too well."[4] Therefore,
in this chapter, we will consider some of God's wondrous attributes for
by carefully pondering them, we will see the Lord in his greatness and
glory and find our confidence fortified and our fears driven away. Such
a renewed perspective will truly enable us to live victoriously in the
midst of a deteriorating culture around us.

For example, in Isaiah 40, the cry of the prophet to the people
of Judah was "Behold your God!" (Isaiah 40:9). Hence, Isaiah speaks
in this stirring chapter of the glory of the Lord (Isaiah 40:5), his eternal Word (Isaiah 40:8), his might in reward and judgment (Isaiah
40:10), his power in creation (Isaiah 40:12, 22, 26), and his wisdom
and understanding (Isaiah 40:13–14, 28). This is the God Isaiah was
calling the people to behold, and it is the God we are to behold! Ken
Gire has penned these poignant words:

Everything in our life finds proper value
once we have properly valued Him. We take

time for what we value. And we behold what we love. It is not the duty of beholding that changes us, though, but rather the beauty of the one we behold.[5]

Were nations threatening Judah in Isaiah's day? Were earthly kings exalting themselves and setting their sights on conquering God's people? The answer was not panic or fleeing or the increase of military might (see Psalm 33:16–20). The answer was for the people to behold their God in his stunning attributes. The antidote to the fears of the people would be a renewed vision of their glorious and all-powerful God.

> Behold, the nations are like a drop from a bucket, and are accounted as the dust on the scales... All the nations are as nothing before him, they are accounted by him as less than nothing and emptiness. (Isaiah 40:15, 17)

We have seen the reality of God's sovereign and providential actions throughout history, and now in more modern times, we have seen it as well. For example, in commenting on Mikhail Gorbachev and the fall of the Soviet Union, Christopher Wright notes that "there is a divine irony, a sense of humor almost, that the grip of communist tyranny in Europe should not be brought down by the might of its enemies but by the policies of its own foremost head of state."[6] As hymnist, William Cowper put it in 1774: "God moves in a mysterious way His wonders to perform."

The point then is that God uses leaders by giving them "temporary ability and power to set in motion processes and events which achieve God's purpose, and when they have fulfilled that role, he then sets them down and moves on. Nobody is indispensable."[7]

The attributes of God can be seen in two categories: those that are unique to God alone (that is, attributes that he does not share with his children) and, secondly, those attributes that God *does* share with them and that they are to reflect in their daily lives. Of course, this is not a comprehensive list of God's attributes in either category; certain ones are simply highlighted for the purpose of this book.

Also, for each of these attributes of God, I am suggesting a corresponding hymn that relates to the meaning of the particular attribute being pondered. Consider using these hymns in your times of personal worship. "Let God speak directly to His people through the Scriptures, and let His people respond with grateful songs of praise."[8]

> Let those refuse to sing
> that never knew our God
> but children of the heavenly King
> may speak their joys abroad.[9]

Thus, as we look at the attributes of God, we can surely sing to him with awe as did Moses, "Who is like you, O Lord, among the gods? Who is like you, majestic in holiness, awesome in glorious deeds, doing wonders?" (Exodus 15:11).

In this chapter, let's consider some of those remarkable attributes that are unique to God alone.

God Is Triune

Hymn: "Come, Thou Almighty King" (Anonymous, circa 1757).

The word *Trinity* means "threeness" (from the Latin term *trinitas*), and although the word is not found in the Bible, the concept of the Trinity is thoroughly biblical. It means that God exists eternally as one being while also existing eternally as three united persons: Father, Son, and Holy Spirit (Luke 1:35, 3:21–22; 2 Corinthians 13:14). In the very first verse of the Bible, the term for *God* is *Elohim* and is in a plural form. Thus, each of the divine persons is fully God, having one divine essence.

Deuteronomy 6:4 declares, "Hear, O Israel: The Lord our God, the Lord is one." This great statement became the Jewish confession of faith as faithful Jews recited it morning and evening. Furthermore, the Hebrew word for *one* in this statement does not mean *singleness*.

42

It means *unity* and is the same word used in Genesis 2:24 where husband and wife become "one flesh." So while Deuteronomy 6:4 is a great declaration of the oneness of God, it does not negate the concept of the Trinity.

Also, in Genesis 1:26, God refers to himself in plural terms, saying, "Let us make man in our image, after our likeness." At the same time, Scripture is clear that there are not three Gods but only one. For example, in Matthew 28:19, we read the words, "Baptizing them in the name of the Father and the Son and the Holy Spirit." The triune name here is singular (not "names") for there is one God who exists in three distinct persons, each of whom is eternal and equal in majesty and power.

An ancient Trinitarian expression seeks to communicate the historic Christian understanding of this doctrine: The Father is not the Spirit; the Father is not the Son. The Son is not the Father; the Son is not the Spirit. The Spirit is not the Father; the Spirit is not the Son. The Father is God; the Spirit is God; the Son is God.

Consider also these excerpts from the Athanasian Creed (circa mid-fifth century), written to provide vitally important clarification on biblical teaching about the Trinity:

> For the person of the Father is a distinct person, the person of the Son is another, and that of the Holy Spirit still another. But the divinity of the Father, Son, and Holy Spirit is one, the glory equal, the majesty coeternal... None in this Trinity is before or after, none is greater or smaller; in their entirety the three persons are coeternal and coequal with each other.[10]

It should come as no surprise that the doctrine of the Trinity has perplexed countless minds over the centuries. For example, the great fifth-century theologian and Christian leader Augustine spent much time thinking about this doctrine. One day, as he walked along the seashore, he saw a boy digging in the sand. He stopped and asked the boy what he was trying to do, and the child replied that he wanted to empty the sea into his hole in the sand. This caused Augustine to begin thinking, *Am I not trying to do the same thing as this child, in seeking to exhaust with my reason the infinity of God and to collect it within the limits of my own mind?*[11]

There are, of course, many things we won't be able to comprehend about God because, like Augustine, we will never be able to put an infinite God into our finite minds. It simply cannot be done. In fact, because God is infinite even throughout eternity, "we will never exhaust the depths of His being or the way in which He exists as both One and Three."[12]

> For my thoughts are not your thoughts, neither are your ways my ways, declares the Lord. For as the heavens are higher than the earth, so are my ways higher than your ways and my thoughts than your thoughts. (Isaiah 55:8–9)

Nevertheless, over the years, a number of analogies have been offered in an attempt to explain or illustrate the Trinity. However, due to the majesty and mystery involved in this doctrine and to the limitations of our human thinking, all such analogies will inevitably fall short. Stuart Olyott put it like this:

> There is no way we can picture this truth. You can have three men, each of whom is equally human, and distinct from the other. But at the end of the day you will have three men and not one. The three persons of the Godhead are each equally God, and distinct from each other. The mystery is that you still have but one God.[13]

Now being unable to resolve the difficulties in the doctrine of the Trinity is "in one sense," as Bruce Milne points out, "Entirely predictable since God is the transcendent Lord of all being. Indeed, if we did not encounter deep mystery in God's nature there would be every reason for suspicion concerning the Bible's claims."[14]

Thus, the Trinity is not a matter for debate nor even a matter for attempted explanation since to a great degree, the Trinity is incomprehensible to the mind of man. We simply must have a reverent acceptance of this essential doctrine taught in the Bible. Author Christian George writes with perception and a touch of humor:

> We are living in an age when we know that the more we know, the more we know that we don't know much at all. You know? And such knowledge makes us small again... We understand the Trinity as much as ants understand airplanes—it's way over our heads. We embrace the mystery of the Trinity because it has embraced us.[15]

At the same time, it is important to understand that although the Trinity is a mystery, it is not a contradiction. "While the Trinity may go beyond reason, it does not go against reason."[16]

Now while there is much we cannot fully grasp about the nature of God, it is also true that there is much he has revealed in his Word about his personhood and purposes. For example, several times in Scripture all three divine persons are present and operating at the same time: The first verse of the Bible declares that God created the heavens and the earth (Genesis 1:1). Scripture also reveals that he did it through his Son (Colossians 1:16; Hebrews 1:2), and in Genesis 1:2, it is clear that the Holy Spirit was involved in creation as well.

Concerning Mary, the mother of Jesus, the Bible teaches that the Holy Spirit came upon her, the power of God overshadowed her, and the child she conceived was the Son of God (see Luke 1:35). All three persons of the Trinity were present. Furthermore, at the baptism of Jesus, the Father acknowledged the Son, and the Holy Spirit descended on the Son, empowering him for ministry (see Mark 1:9–11).

Lastly, we see the work of the triune God in our own salvation: the Father chose us in Christ (Ephesians 1:4; John 6:37, 44), the Son redeemed us through his atoning death (Romans 5:6–8; Ephesians

1:7), and the Holy Spirit sealed our salvation (John 3:5–8; Ephesians 1:13, 4:30).

It is no wonder then that the apostle Peter shows the immense encouragement the doctrine of the Trinity brings believers when he addresses his letter to the "elect exiles" and says, "According to the foreknowledge of God the Father, in the sanctification of the Spirit, for obedience to Jesus Christ and for sprinkling with his blood: May grace and peace be multiplied to you" (1 Peter 1:1–2).

It's important to understand that Peter wrote his letter to Christians under severe persecution in the Roman Empire; therefore, his strong doctrinal emphasis would focus their minds on divine truth and strengthen their hearts in their triune God. May the same Trinitarian emphasis do the same for us in a day of cultural insanity with its attendant threat to religious freedom and free speech.

Thus, while there is certainly divine mystery involved in the nature of the Trinity, it is a magnificent doctrine that should continually move our hearts in praise to God. Sam Storms identifies the right perspective for all of us:

> I freely concede that the best and most enlightened minds in the Christian world reach a point in their exploration of the Trinity where they simply throw up their hands, not so much in frustration but in awe and wonder and worship at so glorious and majestic a God![17]

May we do the same as we contemplate the mystery and the majesty of the Trinity!

> To Thee, great One in Three,
> The highest praises be,
> Hence evermore;
> Thy sov'reign majesty
> May we in glory see,
> And to eternity
> Love and adore.[18]

God Is Eternal

Hymn: "Praise, My Soul, the King of Heaven" (words by Henry F. Lyte, 1834).

An undeniable lesson of history is that things on earth don't last forever. Just think of the great civilizations that have fallen, and all that is left of those ancient kingdoms are the ruins (and a lot of sand).

Yet while the things of earth will fade away, the Creator of all things will last forever. The psalmist prayed, "Lord, you have been our dwelling place in all generations. Before the mountains were brought forth, or ever you had formed the earth and the world, from everlasting to everlasting you are God" (Psalm 90:1–2).

In 1 Timothy 1:17, Paul says that God is immortal. Thus, both the Old and New Testaments clearly teach that God is eternal in his being; he is without beginning and without ending. Go back as far as you want, God will be there. Go forward as far as you want, God will be there. He lives forever.

> There never was
> When God was not;
> There never will be
> When God will not be.[19]

Therefore, God creates, but he was never created. He causes, but he was never caused. Since no act brought him into being, none can take him out.

Back in the 1960s, there was a "God is dead" movement. Happily, the movement is dead! And God lives on. His existence is from eternity past and extends into eternity future.

> "I am the Alpha and the Omega," says the
> Lord God, "who is and who was and who is to
> come, the Almighty." (Revelation 1:8)

So who but unbelieving, liberal theologians would come up with the idea that the eternal God had died? Did they miss the word *eternal*? C. S. Lewis said that all that is not eternal is eternally out of date. Obviously then, those unbelieving theologians from the '60s were eternally out of date—though they perhaps considered themselves on the cutting edge of theological erudition!

Now with our finite minds, we may struggle to understand the eternality of God. After all, how do we get our head around the fact that he is without beginning? We can't...but we don't have to. We simply rejoice in what Scripture tells us about God's greatness and eternal nature.

Evelyn Underhill said that if God were small enough to be understood, he wouldn't be big enough to be worshipped. Yes, God is indeed beyond our understanding. Therefore, because he is who he is, he deserves our continual worship. Rick Cornish gives a clear summary of the eternality of God and what our response to it should be:

> God eternally exists, complete and self-sufficient. He didn't create the world to fill a need in Himself. He doesn't depend on the universe or us to fill any lack within Himself. No other deserves worship, praise, and adoration. God did not begin; He will not end; He simply is, and we should praise Him for it.[20]

Now let's think about how this attribute of God relates to the gospel. When Jesus died on the cross to save us from our sins, it seemed as if his life had ended. Yet because of the eternal nature of his divine being, he was raised from the dead and will never die again. As Hebrews 13:8 says, "Jesus Christ is the same yesterday and today and forever."

Therefore, because God is eternal, he is able to guarantee eternal life to those who come to him through Jesus Christ. That's the good news of the gospel—that all who believe in the eternal Christ will receive eternal life. Thus, the only sensible thing for people to do who are without Christ is to truly believe in him, and all who do so will not be turned away. In John 5:24, Jesus says, "Truly, truly, I say to you, whoever hears my word and believes him who sent me has eternal life. He does not come into judgment, but has passed from death to life."

Furthermore, as our eternal God and everlasting King (Jeremiah 10:10), the Lord will lead us, care for us, and comfort us throughout all of life. Then one day, he will usher us into his presence in heaven where we will be with him forever. David prayed, "Your kingdom is an everlasting kingdom, and your dominion endures throughout all generations" (Psalm 145:13; see also Daniel 7:13–14). The greatness of God is truly beyond description, and his eternal kingdom is one of infinite glory and majesty.

Moreover, in Matthew 13, Jesus compares the kingdom of heaven to a great treasure (Matthew 13:44) and to a pearl of great price (Matthew 13:46). Thus, to be in the kingdom is everything, but to be outside the kingdom is worse than anything we might imagine.

The good news is that the door to the kingdom is open to all. We don't have to be rich to enter Christ's kingdom. We don't have to be powerful or beautiful or clever. God's kingdom is not like some elite club where you have to know the right people to get in. If certain clubs or organizations won't have us, why would that matter if we are in the kingdom of God...and in it for eternity? For when all our earthly dreams have turned to dust and blown away in the wind, God's kingdom will remain. His kingdom is eternal because *he* is eternal. Therefore, let us rejoice in his eternality and proclaim this truth to others.

People criticized a certain archbishop because he "did not preach to the times." His reply was spot-on: "While so many are preaching to the times, may not one poor brother preach for eternity?"[21] Indeed, there is a desperate need in our day for more brothers to preach for eternity!

Let us determine then as preachers and laypeople alike to live and communicate the truth with a sense of urgency and always with eternity in view. The gospel message we proclaim is life-changing now...and forever!

God Is Unchanging

Hymn: "Great Is Thy Faithfulness" (words by Thomas O. Chisholm, 1923).

We have been hearing for some time now that we live in a post-Christian America, and, of course, there is much evidence that this is true. One might also wonder if the post-Christian America has now become a post-*sanity* America! Is this not true—at least on a number of levels—in light of massive shifts in social, moral, and cultural thinking and behavior taking place in our nation?

The good news is that in this sea of enormous societal change, there is one who *never* changes! The Bible declares, "Every good and perfect gift is from above, coming down from the Father of lights, who does not change like shifting shadows" (James 1:17 CSB). We confess with the psalmist:

> Of old you laid the foundation of the earth, and the heavens are the work of your hands. They will perish, but you will remain; they will all wear out like a garment. You will change them like a robe, and they will pass away, but you are the same, and your years have no end. (Psalm 102:25–27)

These words bring great perspective and encouragement to our hearts in the midst of the constant, unrelenting change all around us. It's been said that the more things change…the more things change! However, the one who does *not* change is God himself (Malachi 3:6); he is the one constant in whom we have an unfailing anchor for our souls (Hebrews 6:17–19).

Why is God unchanging? Arthur Pink gives the answer to that question: "He cannot change for the better, for he is already perfect; and being perfect, he cannot change for the worse."[22] This is a vitally important reality to remember in a day like ours—with so much change happening in our culture and much of it immoral and destructive. Yet when everything nailed down seems to be coming up, God remains the same.

Here's more good news: Because God himself is unchanging, he has produced an unchanging Word. The truth of Scripture is not only *timely* for our day; it is also *timeless*, which means that it is relevant and applicable to every generation and nation and people group.

In April of 1991, a man by the name of Sergei Krikalev was living in what was then Leningrad, Russia, and earning five hundred rubles a month. He believed in the Communist party and endorsed the leadership of Mikhail Gorbachev while dismissing Boris Yeltsin as a political nobody.

Krikalev was a Russian cosmonaut who was shot into space as part of the Soviet space program. Due to events beyond his control, his five-month journey stretched into ten months before he landed back on earth. When he returned, Krikalev entered a new world called the Commonwealth of Independent States. The old Soviet Union had come apart at the seams. His hometown of Leningrad was renamed St. Petersburg, Gorbachev had become a capitalist signing million-dollar book deals, and the "insignificant" Yeltsin was now the president of Russia.

The Communist party had lost its power, and Krikalev's five-hundred-rubles-a-month salary couldn't even purchase a pair of scissors to cut the USSR insignia off his tattered uniform. In less than a year and without warning while Sergei Krikalev circled the earth, a new era began.[23]

Likewise, new eras have burst upon us as massive cultural changes have engulfed our own nation. Yet our hope is in the God who does *not* change. As the great Puritan writer Stephen Charnock put it, "God always is what he was, and always will be what he is."[24]

> Swift to its close ebbs out life's little day;
> Earth's joys grow dim, its glories pass away;
> Change and decay in all around I see:
> O Thou who changest not, abide with me![25]

God Is Sovereign

Hymn: "O Father, You Are Sovereign" (words by Margaret Clarkson, 1982).

The sovereignty of God refers to his absolute rule and authority. Thus, despite appearances, he controls nations, global events, world leaders, and natural disasters. In fact, he is in control of *all* things, carrying out his will perfectly and sovereignly. He is, as Arthur Pink puts it, "unrivalled in majesty, unlimited in power, unaffected by anything outside himself."[26] King David's prayer in 1 Chronicles 29 powerfully expresses the sovereignty of Almighty God:

> Blessed are you, O Lord, the God of Israel our father, forever and ever. Yours, O Lord, is the greatness and the power and the glory and the victory and the majesty, for all that is in the heavens and in the earth is yours. Yours is the kingdom, O Lord, and you are exalted as head above all. Both riches and honor come from you, and you rule over all. In your hand are power and might, and in your hand it is to make great and to give strength to all. And now we thank you, our God, and praise your glorious name. (1 Chronicles 29:10–13)

In stark contrast to this inspiring prayer of David are those who would deny the truth of God's sovereignty; they are, in effect, declaring independent ownership of their lives. In essence, they are putting themselves in the place of God, seeking to govern their lives according to their own self-serving desires. The world, of course, is full of such self-deification. This is why people speak of "my truth" and why some—if they are not content with their biological sex—will seek to transition to the opposite sex. They are taking on the role of God, thinking that they know better than their Creator!

Moreover, if there is *any* sin in our lives (overt or otherwise) of which we refuse to repent, we are declaring ourselves to be our own sovereign even if we never give voice to such a reality. However, the true God—who is perfectly holy and the only one worthy of worship—will never share his glory with another (Isaiah 42:8).

> Remember the former things of old; for I am God, and there is no other; I am God, and there is none like me, declaring the end from the beginning and from ancient times things not yet done, saying, "My counsel shall stand, and I will accomplish all my purpose." (Isaiah 46:9–10)

Furthermore, the truth of God's sovereignty brings immense joy and comfort to believers as they rest in the fact that he will carry out his divine will in his perfect timing and all for his glory alone. Nothing and no one can destroy or thwart his purposes. He is truly sovereign over all—even the weather, as Isaac Watts clearly understood:

> There's not a plant or flower below
> But makes Thy glories known;
> And clouds arise and tempests blow
> By order from Thy throne.[27]

Therefore, we should especially cling to the magnificent truth of God's sovereignty in the midst of suffering. For the reality is that because God is sovereign, he is in control of suffering and uses it to deepen our lives and bring glory to himself. Thus, we can sing with absolute confidence: "When all around my soul gives way, He then is all my hope and stay."[28]

You may never understand why certain things happen, but you can trust the God who is over it all and in control of it all. You can rest in him and his protection, not because you understand what is happening, but because you know the One who is in charge of what is happening to you. Thus, believers who acknowledge and rejoice in the sovereignty of God need not fear the future for they know the one who planned it and controls it.

Through the prophet Jeremiah, God encouraged the Jewish exiles by saying, "For I know the plans I have for you, declares the Lord, plans for welfare and not for evil, to give you a future and a hope" (Jeremiah 29:11). Always remember that which God plans, he carries out perfectly. As he promised a future and a hope to the exiles, he has promised a future and a hope to us through Jesus Christ—not just for this life but for eternity! The psalmist declared, "For the Lord God is a sun and shield; the Lord bestows favor and honor. No good thing does he withhold from those who walk uprightly" (Psalm 84:11).

Yes, these are unprecedented times (at least for our generation). However, I have come to believe that the word *uncertain* is the wrong one to use in describing the day in which we live. Clearly, these are uncertain times for the world, but they are not uncertain for believers; our lives are in the hands of our Creator and Redeemer no matter what happens in this world. We have a God-given certainty and security in Jesus Christ (Colossians 3:1–4).

Thus, the fears and anxieties of life are not calmed by superficial solutions. They are not calmed by the latest philosophy or ideology being peddled in our day. They are not calmed by accepting politically correct positions so we can be on the "right side of history." No, life's concerns and fears are calmed by acknowledging that God is in *charge* of history and, subsequently, by trusting in him with all our hearts. Therefore, it is a marvelous privilege to recognize and humbly bow before our majestic God—the one who is eternally sovereign!

Consider carefully these encouraging words from Elliot Clark as we seek to navigate the perilous times in which we live:

> Hope for the Christian isn't just confidence in a certain glorious future. It's hope in a present providence. It's hope that God's plans can't be thwarted by local authorities or irate mobs, by unfriendly bosses or unbelieving husbands, by Supreme Court rulings or the next election. The Christian hope is that God's purposes are so unassailable that a great thunderstorm of events

can't drive them off course. Even when we're wave-tossed and lost at sea, Jesus remains the captain of the ship and the commander of the storm.[29]

Yes, that's sovereignty! The apostle Paul certainly understood this attribute of God and was encouraged by it as he experienced perilous times in his day. God said to him in Corinth where Paul was facing opposition, "Do not be afraid, but go on speaking and do not be silent, for I am with you, and no one will attack you to harm you, for I have many in this city who are my people" (Acts 18:9–10).

Furthermore, as we study God's Word, we realize that he is at work in the midst of *all* our days, both the joyous and the challenging, the peaceful and the tumultuous. Think of it: we are in the hands of the sovereign Creator who perfectly works out his purposes through every detail of our lives. We often hear it said that the devil is in the details. No, it is God himself who is in the details. Every one of them!

> The fictitious power of chance
> and fortune I defy.
> My life's minutest circumstance
> is subject to his eye.[30]

What a strong sense of security this understanding of God's sovereign control over every detail of our lives gives to us! Furthermore, this reality also encourages us in our places of service for him in that we can rejoice with confidence that we are where we are not because we were appointed by any individual or group but because we are under the divine appointment of God himself.

Thus, the sovereignty of God gives us a perspective on life and eternity that far surpasses all humanistic philosophies and worldviews for we are not under the control of tyrannical governments, sudden plagues, and natural disasters. We are under God's control.

Therefore, because of this incontestable reality, all of creation answers to him and his commands—every day, for all time.

> This is my Father's world;
> O, let me not forget
> that though the wrong
> seems oft so strong,
> God is the Ruler yet.[31]

Note Paul's climactic statement in Romans 11—a statement that powerfully and succinctly declares the sovereignty of God: "For from him and through him and to him are all things. To him be glory forever. Amen" (Romans 11:36). Pastor and author Scotty Smith writes:

> How desperately our generation of Christians needs a fresh vision and understanding of the sovereignty of God. We are not fatalists. Patty Page [Doris Day] is not our patron theological saint as she sang, "Que sera, sera, whatever will be, will be." Neither are we stoics, who brace ourselves against the storms of life and accept all things with passive resignation. Neither must we allow ourselves to become superficial evangelicals, full of denial about the reality of pain and suffering, groping for one more biblical Band-Aid and spiritual anesthetic to deal with huge and troubling issues which are an inevitable part of the Christian life.[32]

Our generation is in desperate need of this kind of vision—that of the sovereign, majestic, triune God who is infinitely superior over all his creation. It is the vision of an occupied throne in heaven (Revelation 4–5) upon which God rules and reigns forever (Revelation 19:6)!

Author and philosopher Jean Paul Richter has been quoted as saying these memorable words about Christ, "He, the holiest among the mighty, and the mightiest among the holy, has lifted with His pierced hands empires off their hinges, has turned the stream of centuries out of its channel, and still governs the ages."

Yes, as the risen Lord, he continues to govern the ages. He always has and always will. In this, we have unshakable hope. Therefore, let us daily express our love in wholehearted worship, devotion, and thanksgiving to our sovereign Creator, Redeemer, and Sustainer.

God Is All-Powerful

Hymn: "I Sing the Mighty Power of God" (Isaac Watts, 1715).

As the Creator and Giver of life, God has displayed his omnipotence, and as the one true God, he is to be worshipped by all of creation.

> You are the Lord, you alone. You have made
> heaven, the heaven of heavens, with all their host,
> the earth and all that is on it, the seas and all that
> is in them; and you preserve all of them; and the
> host of heaven worships you. (Nehemiah 9:6)

Daniel 4 records the experience of Nebuchadnezzar, the king of Babylon, who was quite full of himself and, consequently, judged by God for his extreme pride. However, once the king was humbled and brought to his senses, he said this about the Lord:

> His dominion is an everlasting dominion,
> and his kingdom endures from generation to
> generation; all the inhabitants of the earth are
> accounted as nothing, and he does according to
> his will among the host of heaven and among
> the inhabitants of the earth; and none can stay
> his hand or say to him, "What have you done?"
> (Daniel 4:35)

Yes, God is all-powerful. We know this through creation itself, which, of course, was brought into existence by his power and continues to be sustained by his power. For example, we know that the earth is 25,000 miles in circumference, weighs 6 septillion and 588 sextillion tons, and hangs unsupported in space! King David may not have known these figures, but he certainly had it right when he declared that "power belongs to God" (Psalm 62:11).

We could also consider the unimaginable vastness of space. We have knowledge of about one hundred billion stars in our galaxy. However, there are billions more galaxies that are billions of light-years away! Thus, the sheer immensity of the universe points unmistakably to the sovereign glory and power of the Creator. Little wonder David declared, "The heavens declare the glory of God" (Psalm 19:1).

Yet, amazingly, many people are enamored with their *own* power. They remind us of those described in Psalm 2 who set themselves against the Lord and his anointed, saying, "Let us burst their bonds apart and cast away their cords from us" (Psalm 2:3). God's response to such arrogance and folly is seen in the next verse: "He who sits in the heavens laughs." Thus, Christian George quips, "Our planet is the comedy club for the solar system. The heavens declare the glory of God, but we declare our own glory."[33] How could anything be more breathtakingly foolish than for humans to declare their own glory? Ponder the declarations of Scripture:

> I form light and create darkness; I make well-being and create calamity; I am the Lord, who does all these things. (Isaiah 45:7)

> He makes nations great, and he destroys them; he enlarges nations, and leads them away. (Job 12:23)

> I know that you can do all things, and that no purpose of yours can be thwarted. (Job 42:2)

Yes, only a mind closed to the obvious will deny the clear evidence that God is all-powerful. Such individuals (and nations) would do well to grasp the truth of what Isaac Watts penned so long ago:

> Before Jehovah's awesome throne
> Ye nations, bow with sacred joy;
> Know that the Lord is God alone;
> He can create; and He can destroy.

Moreover, God's omnipotence is displayed in all of life. For example, who designed the lion to roar, the duck to quack, the dog to bark, and the whale to "sing"? Furthermore, it was God who took a lump of clay, formed a man, stamped his image upon him, and brought him forth as a living being.

Then supremely, in the fullness of time (Galatian 4:4), God clothed himself in human flesh so that in the person of his Son, he might live a perfect life on this earth, die an atoning death on the cross, and rise victoriously from the grave. God is all-powerful!

So is there anything God *cannot* do? Actually, the answer is yes. The Bible teaches us that he cannot lie. He cannot break a promise. He cannot change, as we've already noted. Thus, when it comes to God's omnipotence, we can say it like this: he can do anything he *desires* to do (see Job 23:13). After all, if God did something he did not desire to do, he would be going against his own perfect knowledge and wisdom—an action he would never undertake. As Psalm 135:6 says, "Whatever the Lord pleases, he does."

Thus, because of his omnipotence, God is able to do all his holy will. He leaves nothing undone he desires to do, and he does not do anything unless he desires to do it. Arthur Pink put it like this: "God does as he pleases, only as he pleases, always as he pleases."[34]

The omnipotence of God is a magnificent attribute and brings indescribable comfort to the heart of believers. We know that friends and loved ones can offer help and comfort when we are in the midst of a personal storm. However, our greatest need is for a God who can *still* the storm. Fellow believers in Christ can bless us with their presence when we are dying, but the one who helps us most is the

God who conquered the grave! Truly, the power of God is beyond description.

> Even to your old age I am he, and to gray
> hairs I will carry you. I have made, and I will
> bear; I will carry and will save. (Isaiah 46:4)

Furthermore, because of God's omnipotence, we can trust him to do what is humanly impossible in the ministries he gives us. For example, it is reported that on missionary Robert Morrison's first voyage to China, the captain of the ship asked him, "Do you expect to convert China?"

Morrison replied, "No, but I expect God will."[35]

Exactly. It is God himself who changes individuals and nations. We're thankful that he uses us, but he's the one who accomplishes his purposes through everything that happens—the good and the bad. He is all-powerful.

Therefore, let us confess to him the stunning truth of his omnipotence, meditate on the countless displays of this reality, give him wholehearted worship, and proclaim his wondrous works throughout all of life. Say to God:

> How awesome are your deeds! So great is
> your power that your enemies come cringing to
> you. (Psalm 66:3)

> I will remember the deeds of the Lord; yes,
> I will remember your wonders of old. I will pon-
> der all your work, and meditate on your mighty
> deeds. (Psalm 77:11–12)

> Worthy are you, our Lord and God, to
> receive glory and honor and power, for you cre-
> ated all things, and by your will they existed and
> were created. (Revelation 4:11)

One generation shall commend your works
to another, and shall declare your mighty acts.
(Psalm 145:4)

God Is All-Knowing

Hymn: "What God Ordains Is Always Good" (Samuel
Rodigast, 1675; translated *The Lutheran Hymnal*, 1941).

The Bible reveals that God is omniscient (all-knowing). He
knows the number of hairs on our heads (Luke 12:7) and the number of stars in the universe (Psalm 147:4). Thus, he never looks for
information; he never learns anything. How could God learn something if he already knows it? There is absolutely nothing God does
not know. "Has it ever occurred to you that nothing ever occurs to
God?"[36] The fact is that he knows *all* things...and has *always* known
them.

Moreover, on the basis of God's omniscience, he created all
things with perfect skill. The psalmist declares, "Great is our Lord,
and abundant in power; his understanding is beyond measure"
(Psalm 145:7). The apostle John writes, "Whenever our heart condemns us, God is greater than our heart, and he *knows everything*" (1
John 3:20, emphasis mine).

> Earth from afar has heard Thy fame,
> And worms have learned to lisp Thy name;
> But, O! the glories of Thy mind
> Leave all our soaring thoughts behind.[37]

Moreover, Psalm 139:1–6 speaks powerfully to the truth of
God's omniscience. This stands to reason, of course, in that a being
who existed before anything and created everything would not only
be all-powerful but also all-knowing—utilizing perfect knowledge to
bring about the kind of order and balance we see in the universe, as
well as in the design and functions of the human body.

Psalm 139 is a remarkable psalm as it develops the theme of
being known by God. Thus, all through David's psalm, we see

God's perfect knowledge of our lives—knowledge of all our days even before we were born. David prays in verse 16, "Your eyes saw me when I was formless; all my days were written in your book and planned before a single one of them began" (Psalm 139:16 CSB). It has been reported that, in reflecting on this stunning truth, Charles Spurgeon said: "He knew me before I knew myself; yea, he knew me before I *was* myself."

Some time ago, one of my grandchildren said to me, "Papa, you're old." Did the child's eyes need to be tested? No, I think not! Besides, my grandchild's comment does not bother me for the simple reason that I am the exact age I am *supposed* to be. So are you. Our all-knowing God has planned every detail of our lives. This is not fatalism. It is the reality of an eternal, sovereign God—perfect in knowledge and infinite in power. As a result, we rejoice that he who knows all things knows every detail of our own lives.

On the other hand, such perfect knowledge on the part of our Creator should cause grave distress for unrighteous people. "The eyes of the Lord are in every place, keeping watch on the evil and the good" (Proverbs 15:3). The apostle Peter says that "the face of the Lord is against those who do evil" (1 Peter 3:12), and the apostle Paul refers to the coming day "when God judges what people have kept secret" (Romans 2:16, see also verse 5).

Charles Spurgeon told about a man who asked him, "Can you explain the seven trumpets of the Revelation?"

"No," Spurgeon said, "but I can blow one in your ear and warn you to escape from the wrath to come."[38]

Nothing can be hidden from God. He is all-knowing.

Now think about God's omniscience in relation to your own life. For example, do you rejoice in the fact that his knowledge is perfect and that he will always lead you in the right way? Although God has certainly revealed in his Word that he has infinite knowledge and understanding, we may be in the midst of a trial of some kind and be tempted to think: *Does God really know what I'm going through? Does he care?* However, why would we ever think that way if we believe what God has told us in Scripture concerning his omniscience?

Another passage in Psalm 139 speaks to this very truth. In verses 17–18, we read, "How precious to me are your thoughts, O God! How vast is the sum of them! If I would count them, they are more than the sand. I awake, and I am still with you."

The story is told of a man in England who boasted all his life that King George IV once spoke to him. Of course, the only thing the king said was "Get out of the road!" But it was the king himself who said it, so apparently, it didn't really matter to the man *what* the king said.[39]

As believers, however, we can rejoice that the God of this universe knows us personally, loves us deeply, and thinks of us continually—such is his everlasting love for his people. Furthermore, in Isaiah 49:16, God says that we are engraved on the palms of his hands, as if to show how constantly we are before him.

So does God truly know and care about the circumstances we face and the trials we go through? Indeed, he does! Creation shows it, and his Word reveals it even more clearly. The beloved writer Andrew Murray wrote these words during a low time in his life:

> He brought me here. He will keep me here. He will make this trial a blessing. He will bring me out again. Therefore, I am here by God's appointment, in His keeping, under His training, for His time.[40]

God Is Present Everywhere

Hymn: "This Is My Father's World" (words by Maltbie D. Babcock, 1901).

The Bible clearly teaches that God is present with his entire being at all times and in every place. To quote Spurgeon again: "God is everywhere. His circumference is nowhere, but his center is everywhere."[41]

Psalm 139:7–10 declares this stunning reality. "Where shall I go from your Spirit? Or where shall I flee from your presence?" asks David in verse 7. The answer, of course, is nowhere. Jonah found that out the hard way! However, there's no indication that David is wanting to escape the presence of God; he is probably speaking hypothetically as he ponders God's omnipresence.

As finite beings, we are bound by time and space. Most of us have probably made the statement, "I can't be in two places at once." However, God does not have that limitation.

He *can* be in two places at once.

He can be *everywhere* at once.

He *is* everywhere at once.

C. S. Lewis put it like this: "We may ignore, but we can nowhere evade, the presence of God. The world is crowded with him. He walks everywhere incognito."[42]

> Can a man hide himself in secret places so
> that I cannot see him? declares the Lord. Do I
> not fill heaven and earth? declares the Lord.
> (Jeremiah 23:24)

The question was once asked, "Why is there but one God?"

A child answered, "Because God fills every place and there's no room for another one." Perceptive answer indeed!

> While all that borrows life from Thee is ever in
>   Thy care,
> And everywhere that man can be, Thou, God art
>   present there.[43]

Furthermore, although God is certainly present everywhere, we also see the *manifested* presence of God at certain times and in certain places throughout the Bible. When the ark of the covenant was brought into the temple, King Solomon declared in his prayer of dedication, "But will God indeed dwell on the earth? Behold, heaven and the highest heaven cannot contain you; how much less this house that I have built!" (1 Kings 8:27). Solomon's point was that though God's presence would be powerfully made manifest in the temple, a human structure could not possibly contain the omnipresent God! The words of A. W. Tozer speak strikingly to this great truth:

> God is above all things, beneath all things, outside of all things, and inside of all things. God is above, but He's not pushed up. He's beneath, but He's not pressed down. He's outside, but He's not excluded. He's inside, but He's not confined. God is above all things presiding, beneath all things sustaining, outside of all things embracing, and inside of all things filling.[44]

God is truly in every place at all times in the entirety of his being, but he also sovereignly makes his presence known "in different ways in different situations, to bless, warn, comfort, rebuke, reward, or punish."[45]

In summary, God is triune, eternal, unchanging, sovereign, all-powerful, all-knowing, and present everywhere. These are some of the attributes that are unique to God alone.

CHAPTER 4

Pondering the Imponderable (2)

The following are more wondrous attributes of God, but in contrast with the last chapter, they are ones he shares with us as his children and that we are to reflect through our lives. Obviously, our confused and chaotic culture desperately needs to see these characteristics clearly demonstrated in those who know God and desire him to be known to others.

God Is Holy

Hymn: "Holy, Holy, Holy" (words by Reginald Heber, 1826).

The word *holy* means to be set apart. Thus, God is holy in that he is "completely separated from his creation. Being incomparably exalted, he is worthy of worship. He is proclaimed to be 'Holy, holy, holy' (Isa. 6:3), utterly pure and uncorrupted by sin, though he engages with a sinful world (Hab. 1) and acts to render sinners holy (Isa. 6:4–6)."[1]

At the same time, our perfectly holy God has set apart a people for himself and dwells with them, as seen in this wondrously encouraging verse:

> For thus says the One who is high and lifted
> up, who inhabits eternity, whose name is Holy: "I
> dwell in the high and holy place, and also with

him who is of a contrite and lowly spirit, to revive
the spirit of the lowly, and to revive the heart of
the contrite." (Isaiah 57:15)

It is no surprise that the holiness of God is given a tremendous
emphasis in the Bible. In fact, the word *holy* is the one Scripture uses
to describe God more than any other word. Furthermore, to say that
God is holy means more than the fact that he does not sin. That is
true, of course. He is righteous and undefiled; there is no sin in him.
In fact, he *cannot* sin.

His holiness, however, is more than what he does *not* do. It's
who he *is*. Holiness is the very essence of God's being. It is the separation between the Creator and the creature—the infinite distance
between God's deity and our humanity. Yet, amazingly, in love and
grace, he came to us because we could not go to him. In her song of
praise, Mary declared, "For he who is mighty has done great things
for me, and holy is his name" (Luke 1:49).

Thus, as ungodliness seems to continue unabated in our culture, it is vital that we truly fix our gaze on God who is perfectly holy
and worthy of our highest praise. A powerful illustration of this is in
Isaiah 6 where we are told that Uzziah, the king of Judah, had died.
Keep in mind that this king had been on the throne for fifty-two
years! The land had prospered greatly under his leadership, and the
people had felt quite secure. Now that the king was dead, they were
thrown into turmoil; it was an extremely unsettling time for them.

When the news of Uzziah's death had reached the prophet
Isaiah, he entered the temple in grief and sorrow to seek the Lord
and wait before him. While there, he had an overwhelming vision
of God in his holiness. Isaiah says in verse 1, "In the year that King
Uzziah died I saw the Lord sitting upon a throne, high and lifted up;
and the train of his robe filled the temple."

Think of the significance of those four words: *I saw the Lord.*
How could you ever be the same after an experience like that? The
term used here for *Lord* is *Adonai,* and it is God's supreme title. It
signifies ownership or rulership.

So in the midst of a most distressing situation in the nation, Isaiah saw a vision of God that literally changed his life. He saw the God of heaven reigning, and everything else paled in comparison. Think of it: the throne of Judah may be empty, but the throne of heaven is occupied! Always has been…always will be for security is not in a man. It is in *Adonai*, the God who reigns!

Isaiah saw God as only God is—on the throne, in control, high, and lifted up. So why be filled with panic that the earthly king has died if the heavenly one is still in charge?

Furthermore, Isaiah saw the Lord *sitting* upon a throne (Isaiah 6:1). That's significant! God is not pacing back and forth, wringing his hands. He's not struggling or fretting. No, God is *seated*, and that pictures being settled, secure, and in total control. There is absolutely no panic in the throne room of heaven. There may be confusion and unrest on earth, but there is perfect peace in heaven.

This puts matters in perspective, doesn't it? Is there any problem on earth that would seem large to the one sitting on the throne of the universe? Think about your biggest concern in life right now. Is he in control of that? Yes, even that. Furthermore, aren't you glad that the throne of God is never in danger of a military coup? Lucifer tried that once, and it didn't work!

Now Isaiah went on to hear a holy hymn as an order of angelic beings known as the seraphim were calling to one another in antiphonal praise: "Holy, holy, holy is the Lord of hosts; the whole earth is full of his glory!" (Isaiah 6:3). What a mighty crescendo of praise these heavenly beings offered to God. Perhaps the threefold use of the word *holy* points to God as Father, Son, and Holy Spirit. In Reginald Heber's beautiful hymn, God's holiness is connected with his triune being:

> Holy, holy, holy! Merciful and mighty!
> God in three Persons, blessed Trinity![2]

Furthermore, that which overwhelmed Isaiah in the presence of God was a sense of his own sin, and that is what always happens when we see God as he really is. For it is then that we also see ourselves as we really are, and in becoming aware of our own spiritual neediness, we stop comparing ourselves to anyone else.

As a prophet, it was Isaiah's job to call other people to repentance and holiness, which he did. Then he encountered the holy one himself!

Isaiah had *talked* about God's holiness.

He *believed* in it.

He had *preached* it.

Finally, however, he *experienced* it.

Now what was the specific sin Isaiah confessed? It was unholy speech. Think about that for a moment. Isaiah realized that he was a sinner in the one area of life where he was most committed to doing God's work—that of *speaking* God's truth and judgment to others. However, it was only when he came into the light of God's holy presence that Isaiah realized that he, too, was in great spiritual need. For if the lips are unclean, so is the heart. As Isaiah says later in his book, "We have all become like one who is unclean, and all our righteous deeds are like a polluted garment" (Isaiah 64:6).

Thus, out of his brokenness came confession, and as a result, his sin was forgiven and he was recommissioned for God's service. Let us remember then that it was Isaiah's encounter with God's holiness in verses 1–7 that prepared him to volunteer for God's service in verse 8. It was the grace of God that led him from "Woe is me" (Isaiah 6:5) to "Here I am! Send me" (Isaiah 6:8). You could say that Isaiah went into the temple a mourner and came out a missionary!

It's not only obvious in this passage but all through the Bible that God has called his people to be set apart and to progress in holiness (1 Peter 1:13–16); thus, this is an attribute God shares with his children. In Leviticus 20:26, he says, "You shall be holy to me, for I the Lord am holy and have separated you from the peoples, that you should be mine."

When we come to the New Testament, we see the amazing role of the Holy Spirit in our salvation and sanctification. What happens when we truly come to faith in Christ? Yes, we are given assurance of heaven, but that is not all. Donald Whitney insightfully points out what takes place when the Holy Spirit enters a person:

> Just as you bring your human nature with you whenever you enter any place, so whenever the Holy Spirit enters any person, he brings his holy nature with him. The result is that all those in whom the Spirit dwells have new holy hungers and holy loves they did not have prior to having his indwelling presence. They hunger for the holy Word of God, which they used to find boring or irrelevant (1 Pet. 2:2)… Hearts and minds in which the Holy Spirit dwells feel holy longings unknown to them previously. They long to live in a holy body without sin, yearn for a holy mind no longer subject to temptation, groan for a holy world filled with holy people, and earnestly desire to see at last the face of the one the angels call "Holy, holy, holy" (Rev. 4:8).[3]

Therefore, the new desires we have received from the Holy Spirit constantly inspire us to a God-honoring life of holiness. At the same time, we must make sure that we are seeking God himself and not simply a moral lifestyle. For the more we seek him with all our heart, the more we will desire to please him with a holy life—one that will be reflected in our worship, our thoughts, our words, and our actions.

Thus, this is a critically important truth we must never forget: seeking the knowledge of God through his Word motivates us to daily pursue holiness of life while rejecting all that would deter us from such a life. Call to mind Paul's exhortation to the Corinthian believers: "Let us cleanse ourselves from every defilement of body and spirit, bringing holiness to completion in the fear of God" (2 Corinthians 7:1).

The words of Elisabeth Elliot give us the right perspective on God's work in developing this holiness in our lives:

> What happens today—let us be assured of this—is meant, in the purpose of our loving Father, to make us holy in every part. This making saints out of sinners is a lifelong business. One of the things that slow it down is our tendency to react to the happenings instead of responding to the Holder of the happenings. He is at work. He knows what He's doing. He asks us to believe in His thoroughly loving purpose.[4]

Furthermore, Peter declares to the believing recipients of his letter:

> But you are a chosen race, a royal priesthood, a holy nation, a people for his own possession, that you may proclaim the excellencies of him who called you out of darkness into his marvelous light. (1 Peter 2:9)

Yes, it is through holy lives that an unholy generation can see and hear about the excellencies of the God who calls men and women out of great spiritual darkness into his marvelous light through his Son, the Lord Jesus Christ.

God Is True

Hymn: "O Word of God Incarnate" (words by William Walsham How, 1867).

Over thirty-five years ago, Allan Bloom wrote in his book *The Closing of the American Mind*, "There is one thing a professor can be absolutely certain of: almost every student entering the university believes, or says he believes, that truth is relative."[5]

Consequently, it seems that many students over the years have come to believe that finding truth isn't all that important. It's simply the *search* for it that matters. However, that makes about as much sense as saying, "I'm not that interested in *finding* a job. After all, it's just the *search* for one that matters."

Furthermore, for many people, truth is whatever they want it to be; thus, they speak of "my truth" as though they themselves are the arbitrators of what is true and what is not. However, it is of the utmost importance to know the real truth and not be deceived by Satan's lies. As the nineteenth-century American humorist Josh Billings said, "I'd rather know a few things for certain than be sure of a lot of things that ain't so."

Truthfulness is one of God's attributes and means that he never lies but always speaks the truth (Hebrews 6:18). In fact, he *cannot* lie (1 Samuel 15:29; Titus 1:2). God says, "I the Lord speak the truth; I declare what is right" (Isaiah 45:19). Therefore, to define it simply, truth is what God says!

It is indeed a great encouragement to remind ourselves that God is the beginning of all knowledge, the very source of truth. As God incarnate Jesus says, "I am the way, and the truth, and the life. No one comes to the Father except through me" (John 14:6). He was quite unequivocal on the matter, stating directly and unapologetically that he is the only way to the Father in heaven.

Of course, that exclusive claim has been opposed and mocked down through history. For example, during the Roman Empire, when Emperor Alexander Severus heard about Christianity, he placed an image of Christ beside the other gods in his private chapel (just to be safe, I suppose). The Romans at that point did not have a problem with welcoming Jesus into their pantheon of gods, but that which the Romans could *not* understand was why Christians refused to reciprocate. After all, if the emperor was willing to worship Christ, why weren't the Christians willing to worship the emperor?

Yet the early Christians insisted that in order to truly worship Christ at all, they had to worship Christ *only*. Consequently, this belief in the uniqueness of Jesus as the only means of salvation brought much disdain and persecution, as it clearly continues to do so today.

Many people are fond of saying something like this: "It's narrow-minded and dogmatic to say that Jesus is the only way to heaven." Consequently, it seems we have become quite accustomed to the words *narrow* and *dogmatic* being negative terms. However, truth *is* narrow by definition. Just because the Christian faith seems narrow does not mean it is untrue.

So how do you answer a person who rejects John 14:6 and states that it is just not inclusive enough to believe that Jesus is the *only* way to God? You could point out that in other areas of life, we actually do want that which is narrow and dogmatic. For example, we want a dogmatic pilot when we fly. We don't want him to say, "I'm going to try something different today in landing the plane. After all, I don't want to be dogmatic and say that there's only one way to land!" I think we would rise up and say, "Wait! There *is* only one way to land. So don't do something different. Do what you were trained to do. Do the right thing, the safe thing. We want you to land on the runway, not the highway!"

Likewise, the same principle holds true in the medical field. Would anyone want a doctor who prescribes improper medicine just to keep from being considered narrow-minded?

Thus, while people desire knowledge, truth, and preciseness in other areas of life, many of them don't seem to want these things in the most important area of all! How do you explain such thinking? The only explanation I know is that Satan is a deceiver, and he does whatever he can to keep people from the truth. Thus, the fact that their worldview has glaring inconsistencies in it seems lost on them, and, consequently, we have to factor in the treacherous work of our common enemy who seeks to blind people to the truth (2 Corinthians 4:4).

However, if those to whom we converse and witness have an openness to sound reasoning and logic, we can explain to them the nature of truth and why, by definition, it is narrow while at the same time truly liberating!

Moreover, in his high priestly prayer, Jesus prayed, "And this is eternal life, that they know you the only *true* God, and Jesus Christ whom you have sent" (John 17:3, emphasis mine). Jesus also prayed, "Sanctify them in the truth; your word is truth" (John 17:17). Thus, God's Word has no error whatsoever (2 Timothy 3:16). As Proverbs 30:5 declares, "Every word of God proves true." Theologian Paul Enns sums up what it means to say that God is true:

> First, it means He is the true God in distinction to all others; there is none like Him... Second, He is the truth in that His Word and His revelation are reliable... He can be trusted. Third, He knows things as they are; He is the beginning of all knowledge and makes it available to man in order that man may have fellowship with Him.[6]

Therefore, let us pray with David, "Teach me your way, O Lord, that I may walk in your truth" (Psalm 86:11). Such a consistent walk with God in his Word equips the believer to "speak the truth with his neighbor" (Ephesians 4:25) and "to speak that truth in love" (Ephesians 4:15).

It is important then to remember that love without truth would lead us to simply be sentimental, and truth without love would cause us to be judgmental, but truth and love *together* can change the world! Obviously, we live in a culture in urgent need of hearing the truth in love, as hymnist William How has written:

> O Word of God incarnate,
> O wisdom from on high,
> O truth unchanged, unchanging,
> O light of our dark sky![7]

Truth unchanged, unchanging. Yes, speaking the truth in love to a world in grave spiritual peril is the high privilege of every child of God. Furthermore, by God's grace, we can speak it with clarity and boldness. As Pastor Adrian Rogers has said, "It's better to speak truth that hurts and then helps than falsehood that comforts and then kills."[8]

Thus, no matter the condition of the culture in which we live, we must "not fear for God has willed his truth to triumph through us," as Luther put it in his famous hymn.[9] Because of this reality, we can act with courage and keep proclaiming the truth even in a day when, seemingly, that truth is often ignored, despised, or twisted. An old pastor who heard a new, strange doctrine is reported to have said this:

> You say I am not with it.
> My friend, I do not doubt it.
> But when I see what I'm not with,
> I'd rather be without it.[10]

Obviously, this is a day that calls for extraordinary discernment. We must know the truth of God and hold to it unswervingly. Furthermore, we must always remember that the reason God gave us the Scriptures is that we may know him, have fellowship with him, and live in such a way as to be a channel of biblical truth for others.

> Once to every generation
> comes the moment to decide;
> in the clash of truth with falsehood,
> all must choose and all must side.
> On the rock of Christ's salvation
> stands or falls each mortal soul;
> and the choice goes by forever,
> sealed in God's eternal scroll
>
> Saints in every generation
> kept the flame of truth alive;
> in the face of death, defying
> thrones they knew would not survive.
> Heroes of the cross of Jesus

win with him in this our day,
by his blood and by their witness
come and follow in his way!

Christ in every generation
greatest name the world has known;
teachers, thinkers, faiths and cultures
find their goal in him alone.
His the truth and his the kingdom,
at his cross our paths divide;
once to every generation
comes the moment to decide![11]

God Is Love

Hymn: "How Deep the Father's Love" (words by Stuart Townend, 1995).

This wondrous attribute is greatly emphasized throughout the Bible. For example, Psalm 103:8 says, "The Lord is merciful and gracious, slow to anger and abounding in steadfast love." When we come to the New Testament, we see the supreme display of divine love: "But God shows his love for us in that while we were still sinners, Christ died for us" (Romans 5:8). How could we ever fully comprehend the amazing love of the Father in giving his Son for us and the love of the Son in giving himself to die in our place?

Consider the story of preacher and hymnist Charles Wesley who, for many years, had no personal grasp of this amazing love. In fact, he sought to live the Christian life without truly knowing Christ, even departing England for America in the early eighteenth century to serve as a missionary.

Not surprisingly, Wesley found no peace and no success in his work. He was demanding and autocratic and even insisted on baptizing infants not by sprinkling but by immersing them three times in succession. Needless to say, his approach to ministry didn't always go over very well!

Wesley returned to England ill and depressed, but in God's gracious timing, he met the Savior, and his life was dramatically changed. He wrote, "I now found myself at peace with God, and rejoiced in hope of loving Christ." One of his most famous hymns says it all:

> Amazing love! How can it be?
> That Thou, my God, should die for me?[12]

Oh, how could we ever adequately describe God's immeasurable love for us? As the apostle John exclaims, "See what kind of love the Father has given to us, that we should be called children of God; and so we are" (1 John 3:1). The verb *see* or *behold* in this verse is an imperative. Thus, we are being charged to reflect on just how astonishing the Father's love is for us!

> So near, so very near to God,
> I cannot nearer be;
> For in the person of His Son,
> I am as near as He.
> So dear, so very dear to God,
> More dear I cannot be;
> The love wherewith He loves the Son,
> Such is His love to me.[13]

Thus, as Romans 8:15–17 teaches, we are God's adopted children and, as such, heirs of God and fellow heirs with Christ. We may live in an entitlement-saturated culture, but we belong to an inheritance-saturated kingdom—an inheritance not based on any merit of our own but based rather on the magnificent love of God graciously extended to us through Christ alone. "Every adopted child will receive by divine grace the full inheritance Christ receives by divine right."[14]

Moreover, the God of our salvation leads us, blesses us, and rejoices over us. He even *sings* over us loudly (Zephaniah 3:17)! Therefore, in these strange and disquieting times of this age, we can be strongly encouraged for we belong to the Lord and are eternally secure in his love. We can surely pray with the seventeenth-century theologian John Owen:

> Your love is an eternal love, fixed on us before the foundation of the world, before we were or had done, the least good. This thought alone makes all that is within us leap for joy. We prostrate our souls in humble, holy reverence, and rejoice before you with trembling.[15]

Moreover, the love of God is not temporary or sporadic. In Jeremiah 31:3, the Lord says to his people, "I have loved you with an *everlasting* love; therefore I have continued my faithfulness to you" (emphasis mine).

The fact that God's love is everlasting is a wonderfully encouraging truth. While it means that he will never stop loving us, it also means that he has always loved us; everlasting love stretches in both directions. Therefore, the reason God will never *stop* loving us is because he never *started*. You see, if at some point he had started loving us, it would mean that before that point, he did not love us. However, because his love is everlasting, he has *always* loved us and always *will* love us.

> Changed from glory into glory,
> Till in heav'n we take our place,
> Till we cast our crowns before Thee,
> Lost in wonder, love and praise.[16]

People sometimes say that when they go to heaven, they will ask God questions: why this or that happened or why certain things didn't happen. Really? I think we will simply be lost in "wonder, love, and praise." That will be enough!

Therefore, in light of God's boundless, everlasting love lavished on us (albeit completely undeserved on our part). We are to love him with all our being, both publicly and privately, for he is the one true eternal God and worthy of never-ending praise and love!

The composer of our national anthem, Francis Scott Key, also wrote these moving words:

> Lord, with glowing heart I'd praise Thee
> for the bliss Your love bestows,
> For the pard'ning grace that saves me,
> and the peace that from it flows.
> Help, O God, my weak endeavor;
> this dull soul to rapture raise:
> You must light the flame, or never can
> my love be warmed to praise.[17]

Oh, that God lights this flame in each of us! Jesus was once asked which commandment is the most important of all. He answered, "The most important is, 'Hear, O Israel: The Lord our God, the Lord is one. And you shall love the Lord your God with all your heart and with all your soul and with all your mind and with all your strength'" (Mark 12:30). Therefore, remind yourself constantly of God's infinite love and care for you, and then respond in whole-hearted expressions of love, praise, and gratitude to him.

Furthermore, having received that love, we are privileged to share it with others. Jesus said that the second most important commandment is this: "You shall love your neighbor as yourself" (Mark 12:31). What an amazing difference such love can make in a culture of violence, anger, hatred, and vitriol! An unknown writer said, "Loving others and loving God is a package deal. You can't have one without the other."

Furthermore, our love for one another in the body of Christ is the strongest witness we can give to a watching world that we are truly followers of Jesus. He says, "By this all people will know that you are my disciples, if you have love for one another" (John 13:35). Thus, the love of God flowing through us to other believers is a clear and undeniable declaration that we are committed to Jesus as our Lord and Master.

The apostle John writes, "Whoever says he is in the light and hates his brother is still in darkness. Whoever loves his brother abides in the light, and in him there is no cause for stumbling" (1 John 2:9–10, see also 3:14–15, 4:7–8, 20).

Now while it is true that a genuine believer may fail to be loving in words and actions from time to time, the Holy Spirit will bring conviction of sin and move such a one to repentance. Pastor Ron Prosise relates the following story as told by J. Ritchie Smith:

> The English pastor Newman Hall wrote a booklet in the nineteenth century entitled "Come to Jesus" which led many thousand souls to the Savior. Later in life, he became engaged in a theological controversy which grew more bitter with each new stage of the discussion. At length he prepared a paper which he intended to be a crushing and final reply. He closed the argument by an attack that would be irresistible and overwhelming. He showed his opponent no mercy and felt that he had beaten him to the ground. When the paper was finished, he read it to a friend and asked triumphantly, "How do you think I have handled him?"
>
> "Well," said his friend, "you have effectually disposed of him. Have you thought of a title for your paper?"
>
> "No," Hall replied. "Have you anything to suggest?"
>
> His friend answered, "I propose that you call it 'Go to the Devil, by the author of 'Come to Jesus.'"
>
> The paper was never published.[18]

Thus, think once more on the words of Jesus, "By this all people will know that you are my disciples, if you have love for one another" (John 13:35).

In summary, we can say that because of the infinite love of God for us, we are empowered to love him supremely (1 John 4:19), love our neighbor as ourselves (Mark 12:31), and love fellow believers by abiding in the light (1 John 2:10, see also 5:1–2).

God Is Gracious

Hymn: "God of Grace" (words by Keith Getty and Jonathan Rea, 2003).

Over the years, I have heard a number of definitions of grace but none better than the one by theologian Charles Hodge who said that grace is "the overflowing abundance of unmerited love, inexhaustible in God, and freely accessible through Christ."[19]

Moreover, such indescribable grace, lavished on every believer, is due entirely to the gift of eternal salvation purchased for us through the all-sufficient sacrifice of Jesus on the cross.

Yet because many people feel they are doing the best they can, their hope for acceptance with God is based on good works, church attendance, morality, or some other human effort or religious activity. However, when it comes to entering the kingdom of God, one's best is *never* good enough.

Mark Twain quipped, "Heaven goes by favor. If it went by merit, you would stay out and your dog would go in." Now I assume that by *favor* he meant *grace* because that's what grace is—the active favor of God bestowing the greatest gift on us who deserve the greatest punishment. This grace is a wondrous outflow of his love, goodness, and generosity.

Therefore, grace is grace because we don't deserve it and could never earn it. It is also grace because God is the one who initiates it. Apart from him, there is no grace, no enjoyment of his holy love, and no confidence in his eternal and unshakable security. The good news is that "the grace of God has appeared," as the apostle Paul says, referring to Jesus Christ who is grace incarnate (Titus 2:11). Thank God that his grace has appeared! And that it is such that believers are forever secure in his everlasting love.

In fact, God's remarkable, keeping grace is continually seen throughout the Bible. In Genesis, for example, God displayed his grace to the first man and woman after they sinned by providing garments of skins for them in place of the fig leaves they had made for themselves (Genesis 3:21). In so doing, God provided by his grace a covering for Adam and Eve through the death of an animal as a substitute for their sin. Furthermore, this pointed to the ultimate sacrifice of Jesus on the cross to redeem sinners through his substitutionary death.

Yet even before God treated Adam and Eve with the kindness of providing garments for them, he had demonstrated the importance of grace in the creation account. Genesis 2:15 indicates that Adam was created outside of the garden of Eden: "The Lord God took the man and put him in the Garden of Eden to work it and keep it." Matthew Henry's fascinating comment on this verse about Adam is worth considering:

> He lived out of Eden before he lived in it, that he might see that all the comforts of his paradise-state were owing to God's free grace. He could not plead a tenant-right to the garden, for he was not born upon the premises, nor had anything but what he received; all boasting was hereby forever excluded.[20]

The same is true for those who are in Christ. All we have is owing to God's free grace; we have no basis for boasting "in the presence of God" (1 Corinthians 1:29). What a marvel and source of constant wonder and worship that, by his grace, the Lord chose us in Christ!

If anyone ever stood in wonder and amazement at the stunning grace of God, it was John Newton (1725–1807). He had been a hardened slave trader and lived the most ungodly life imaginable. But in God's mercy, this man came to faith in Christ as his Savior, eventually became a pastor and hymn writer, and even preached before the queen of England.

In later years, due to Newton's poor health and failing memory, it was suggested that he retire (at age eighty-two). He responded, "My memory is nearly gone, but I remember two things: that I am a great sinner and that Christ is a great Savior!"

On another occasion, a friend of Newton complained about someone who was resistant to the gospel and was living a life of great sin. The friend said, "Sometimes I almost despair of that man."

Newton replied, "I never did despair of any man since God saved me." Yes, John Newton understood grace. *Amazing* grace. Another hymnist (and friend of Newton) William Cowper expressed his joy of embracing the gospel of grace:

> All my chains at once were broken,
> from my feet my fetters fell,
> and that word in pity spoken,
> snatched me from the gates of hell.
> Grace divine, how sweet the sound,
> sweet the grace that I have found![21]

A seventeenth-century Scottish preacher by the name of David Dickson put it in a helpful and memorable way. He said that "he had taken all his bad deeds and put them in a heap, and taken all his good deeds and put them in another heap, and fled from them both to Jesus."[22]

Yet multitudes have never grasped the crucial necessity of such action. Many people will look at the heap of all their bad deeds and think, *There's too many, and they're too bad. How could God ever forgive all of that?* On the other hand, there are many who look at the heap of all their good deeds and think, *God has to be impressed with all of this. My many good deeds will surely be enough to get me into heaven.* No! Like the Scottish preacher, we must flee from *both* heaps! For a person's good deeds will never gain for him or her acceptance with God and the assurance of heaven.

There's only *one* deed that will get us to heaven, and that work has already been done for us by another—the Lord Jesus Christ. He accomplished this work on the cross by dying that we might live.

He who had no sin took our sin, guilt, condemnation, and punishment so we could be forgiven and receive the gift of eternal salvation. Amazing grace, to be sure! Therefore, our bad deeds (no matter how severe) can ever overrule God's grace if we will respond in genuine repentance and faith in Christ (see 1 Corinthians 15:9–10).

Furthermore, grace doesn't end with conversion; God gives countless demonstrations of his grace throughout our lives. In fact, Spurgeon said that between here and heaven, every minute that the Christian lives will be a minute of grace.

Hymnist Annie Johnson Flint was one who clearly understood the magnificent beauty of grace and its minute-by-minute necessity. Having lost both parents before she was six years of age, Annie was adopted by a childless couple. However, while still in her teen years, she became afflicted with arthritis and was soon unable to even walk. Annie had aspired to be a composer and concert pianist, but when illness deprived her of being able to play the piano, she started writing poetry instead.

Annie set several of her poems to music. In later life, being unable to open her hands, she wrote many of her poems on the typewriter using only her knuckles. Out of her deep affliction has come one of the songs that has blessed great numbers of people in a time of suffering: "He Giveth More Grace." Annie based her words on three Bible promises: "He gives more grace" (James 4:6), "He increases strength" (Isaiah 40:29), and "May mercy, peace, and love be multiplied to you" (Jude verse 2).

Annie Johnson Flint understood the truth that there is a special grace and strength that God gives us in our time of need as we trust in him. So when troubles and trials come upon us, as they surely will, may we know his added grace, increased strength, and multiplied peace. Ponder Annie's moving words:

> He giveth more grace when the burdens grow
> greater;
> He sendeth more strength when the labors
> increase.
> To added affliction He addeth His mercy;
> To multiplied trials, His multiplied peace.

When we have exhausted our store of endurance,
when our strength has failed ere the day is half
    done,
When we reach the end of our hoarded resources,
Our Father's full giving is only begun.

His love has no limit; His grace has no measure.
His power has no boundary known unto men.
For out of His infinite riches in Jesus,
He giveth, and giveth, and giveth again![23]

Yes, God's grace is a necessity all through our lives, and what an unspeakable joy in knowing we have it! Author Jerry Bridges said, "Your worst days are never so bad that you are beyond the reach of God's grace. And your best days are never so good that you are beyond the need of God's grace."[24]

Yet how often we take matters into our own hands rather than drawing on the matchless resources of God; when we do so, the results are lamentable (to say the least). However, what we cannot do ourselves God can empower us to do. That is to say, he will do it *through* us.

Major Ian Thomas said it like this: "You can't. God never said you could. Jesus can. And he always said he would." Oh, that's a whole lot better than the old pop song lyrics, "All I gotta do is act naturally." Spiritual victory does not come in acting naturally but in drawing on God's grace and supernatural power. It's not what I can do. It's what he does. It's all grace...all the time.

Dr. Martyn Lloyd-Jones was certainly correct when he said that the ultimate test of our spirituality is the measure of our amazement at the grace of God. Such amazement will assuredly move us to constant wonder, worship, and thanksgiving for his inexpressible grace in our lives—an exhaustless supply upon which we can daily depend, knowing that he extends undiminishing faithfulness to his children through all of life. John Bunyan declared, "O that my soul were so full of grace that there might be no longer room for even the least lust to come into my thoughts!"[25]

The reality is that we are often compelled to confess to God that we are needy spiritually, mentally, emotionally, and physically. Yet we rejoice and give thanks that he is the one who meets our needs perfectly, compassionately, continually, and all for his glory alone.

Thus, let us thank him supremely for sending his Son in whom we are chosen (Ephesians 1:4) and have become heirs with God and fellow heirs with Christ (Romans 8:17). What grace!

God Is Wise

Hymn: "The Perfect Wisdom of Our God" (Stuart Townend and Keith Getty, 2011).

The wisdom of God is for his own glory and for the benefit of his own people. Unlike human wisdom, it is perfect and never failing. As the apostle Paul wrote: "Oh, the depth of the riches both of the wisdom and of the knowledge of God! How unsearchable his judgments and untraceable his ways!" (Romans 11:33 CSB).

The wisdom of God is undeniably seen in creation: "It is he who made the earth by his power, who established the world by his wisdom, and by his understanding stretched out the heavens" (Jeremiah 10:12).

> O boundless Wisdom, God most high,
> O Maker of the earth and sky,
> who bid'st the parted waters flow
> in heaven above, on earth below.[26]

Thus, God is not only all-knowing; he is also all-wise. Bible teacher Steven Lawson explains the difference between God's knowledge and his wisdom:

> The knowledge of God and His wisdom
> are not interchangeable terms. Divine knowledge
> deals with God's possession of all facts about
> everyone and everything. The wisdom of God

deals with the best use of that knowledge for the highest goal.[27]

It is not only hard to make sense of many global events in our day, it is also hard at times to understand what God is doing in our own lives. For example, we find ourselves in the midst of sudden, unexpected, and distressing circumstances. So we struggle to understand the Lord's purposes, perhaps even asking (or at least thinking), "Where is God in all of this?"

Yet here's what we *can* know...and *must* know. Whatever God is doing, it is wise. It is right. It is always exactly what should be done. As J. M. L. Monsabré has well stated, "If God would concede me his omnipotence for twenty-four hours, you would see how many changes I would make in the world. But if he gave me his wisdom too, I would leave things as they are." Moreover, it is deeply gratifying to know that God *does* give wisdom to his people (Daniel 2:20–21) when they ask for it in faith. In fact, he promises to do so, as we will discuss in chapter 5.

Furthermore, God's wisdom is supremely displayed in the person of his Son, the Lord Jesus Christ, who is "the power of God and the wisdom of God" (1 Corinthians 1:24). The apostle Paul further writes, "And because of him you are in Christ Jesus, who became to us wisdom from God, righteousness and sanctification and redemption" (1 Corinthians 1:30).

God Is Glorious

Hymn: "Glorious Things of Thee Are Spoken" (John Newton, 1779).

This characteristic of God is unique in that his glory is the sum total of all that he is—the expression of his very essence. It has been said that there is no theme more central to the message of Scripture than the glory of God. Theologian J. Gresham Machen put it like this: "The ultimate end of all things that come to pass, including the ultimate end of the great drama of redemption, is found in the glory of the eternal God."[28]

It is not surprising then that throughout Scripture, there is a great emphasis on God's glory. Only God *has* glory, and only God *deserves* glory. Furthermore, our very existence is for his glory.

> I will say to the north, Give up, and to the south, Do not withhold; bring my sons from afar and my daughters from the end of the earth, everyone who is called by my name, *whom I created for my glory*, whom I formed and made. (Isaiah 43:6–7, emphasis mine)

In Ephesians 1, Paul reminds us three times that salvation is for the glory of God. We usually think of salvation in terms of what happens to us, and, of course, we are indeed thankful for the incalculable privilege of becoming children of God through the finished work of Christ. However, we must remember that, above all, the great work of salvation magnifies our gracious God and brings glory to him.

Furthermore, Romans 8:30 says, "These whom he justified he also glorified." Therefore, your salvation and mine are part of God's great eternal plan—and the biblical doctrine of glorification means that he completes his plan in his way, in his timing, and always for his glory.

By the way, do you know what they sing about in heaven? "Worthy are you, our Lord God, to receive glory and honor and power, for you created all things, and by your will they existed and were created" (Revelation 4:11). Furthermore, in Revelation 5:12, the angels declare, "Worthy is the Lamb who was slain, to receive power and wealth and wisdom and might and honor and glory and blessing." There is then no higher purpose in the universe than the glory of God.

Moreover, as believers, we *share* in God's glory—and that's an amazing thought!

> And we all, with unveiled face, beholding the glory of the Lord, are being transformed into the same image from one degree of glory to

another. For this comes from the Lord who is the Spirit (2 Corinthians 3:18).

It is true that God will not give his glory to another (Isaiah 42:8), but we can, by his grace and power, live and worship in such a way as to glorify him. To glorify him means to praise him for who he is in the totality of his perfect attributes.

Ascribe to the Lord the glory due his name;
worship the Lord in the splendor of holiness.
(Psalm 29:2)

To him belong glory and dominion forever
and ever. Amen. (1 Peter 4:11)

Furthermore, we are to bring glory to God in all of life. The apostle Paul writes, "So, whether you eat or drink, or whatever you do, do all to the glory of God" (1 Corinthians 10:31; see also Colossians 3:17). Similarly, the apostle Peter exhorts us to use our gifts in "order that in everything God may be glorified through Jesus Christ" (1 Peter 4:11).

Teach me, my God and King,
in all things Thee to see,
and what I do in anything
to do it as for Thee.[29]

Yes, God is inexpressibly glorious and infinitely worthy to *receive* glory from all of creation. Indeed, the universe declares the glory of God (Psalm 19:1) "and the reason we exist is to see it and be stunned by it and glorify God because of it."[30] Jerry Bridges points to the supreme importance of God's glory:

Our main goal in life should be to glorify God. That is the ultimate goal to which all knowledge should be directed. Regardless of

how helpful an item or body of knowledge may
be to society, if it does not have as its final purpose the glory of God, it remains defective. It is
at best partial and to a degree distorted. It is like
a structure without a foundation, a plant without
a root.[31]

Therefore, determine to know and love the glory of God and
to "let your light shine before others, so that they may see your good
works and give glory to your Father who is in heaven" (Matthew
5:16). What could be more important in a culture that glories in itself
than that of believers bearing witness to the glory of their Creator,
Redeemer, and Sustainer?

JR Vassar has written:

We must glorify most what is most glorious.
We must love most what is most lovely. We must
value supremely what is supremely valuable. The
only way out of thinking too much about our
glory, loveliness, and value is to be captured by a
vision of the glorious, lovely, supremely valuable
God.[32]

Vassar also gives a helpful analogy with which most of us can
identify:

When my annual school yearbook came
out, I would flip to the index, find my name,
and look for all the pages where my picture was.
Sometimes it was a good year, and my picture
was on several pages. Other years I languished in
obscurity, appearing only on the page where my
personal mugshot had been placed. I remember
how happy I was to see my picture on multiple
pages and also how ripped off I felt for buying
the yearbook and finding very few pictures of

myself. But real life is not like a yearbook. God will not make us happy by filling up our world with pictures of ourselves so that we can feel important; that is narcissism. I've realized that God will make me happy by filling up my world with pictures of him so that I lose my preoccupation with myself and feel the wonder and awe for which I am really hungry. The only way to win in this life is to lose the war for glory, to choose what is truly valuable, and to surrender to God the highest place in our hearts.[33]

Let us then set our hearts daily on giving God all the glory for he alone is perfectly glorious; he alone is infinitely worthy of being glorified through our worship and obedience.

> Not to us, O Lord, not to us, but to your name give glory, for the sake of your steadfast love and your faithfulness! (Psalm 115:1)

> Dawn to dusk, from east to west,
> Let the Lord's great name be blessed.
> Over nations lifted high,
> Lord, Your glory crowns the sky!
> Lord, Your glory crowns the sky![34]

Obviously, we could never fully plumb the depths of God's character. In the words of Spurgeon: "As well might a gnat seek to drink in the ocean, as a finite creature to comprehend the infinite God."

By his grace, however, we can know him more fully through studying and meditating on his majestic attributes. Moreover, in gaining a deeper understanding of who God is, we will experience an ever-growing desire to offer him greater fervency in praise and thanksgiving.

> The mercy of God is an ocean divine,

A boundless and fathomless flood.
Launch out in the deep, cut away the shore line,
And be lost in the fullness of God.[35]

What a different perspective we will gain on the challenges of life and the insanity so prevalent in our culture when we launch out in the deep and are lost in the fullness of God! Let me encourage you to read carefully and meditatively King David's magnificent prayer in 1 Chronicles 29:11–14 and make it your own:

> Yours, O Lord, is the greatness and the power and the glory and the victory and the majesty, for all that is in the heavens and in the earth is yours. Yours is the kingdom, O Lord, and you are exalted as head above all. Both riches and honor come from you, and you rule over all. In your hand are power and might, and in your hand it is to make great and to give strength to all. And now we thank you, our God, and praise your glorious name. But who am I, and what is my people, that we should be able thus to offer willingly? For all things come from you, and of your own have we give you.

Notice David's response in verses 13–14 to the majestic truths he has just affirmed about God, not least of which is the fact that he is "our God" (1 Chronicles 29:13). Think of it: this eternal, perfectly holy, glorious Creator and Redeemer is *our God*! Thus, Puritan writer David Clarkson shows the attributes of God to be deeply personal when he prays:

> Lord God, how I thank you because you have given me yourself, and an interest in all your glorious attributes: whatever is in you shall be mine, and for me. Oh, what encouragement to faith: to be assured that all your attributes are

mine; as much mine as the drink in my cup and
the food on my plate. May the hands of my faith
take hold of these two handles: that you are willing and able. For there is no condition into which
I can fall but some divine attribute can support
me.[36]

May the study of God's glorious attributes always lead us to
worship him with our whole heart, demonstrating both theology and
doxology. The truth of his majesty, power, and infinite superiority
over all his creation is seen in these moving lyrics:

> Immortal, invisible, God only wise,
> in light inaccessible hid from our eyes,
> most blessed, most glorious, the Ancient of Days,
> Almighty, victorious, Thy great name we praise.[37]

CHAPTER 5

Promises Too Good to Be True...
If Made by Anyone but God!

People make promises; people break promises. God makes promises and *never* breaks them; he is able to keep what he promises (Numbers 23:19). To say it another way, God is unable to make a promise and *not* keep it, thus demonstrating not only his omnipotence but also the unchangeableness of his being as well. A. W. Pink said that the permanence of God's character guarantees the fulfillment of his promises.

Similarly, the Puritan writer Isaac Ambrose prayed, "Lord...you are as faithful to keep as you are generous to make these precious promises. Your grace is unsearchable."[1] Thus, as Hebrews 10:23 exhorts us, we are to "hold fast the confession of our hope without wavering, for he who promised is faithful."

Corrie ten Boom came to grasp and love this thrilling truth firsthand. Her remarkable story is a stunning illustration of God's powerful promises. Few people would have imagined any good coming out of her being incarcerated during World War II as prisoner 66730 in a Nazi concentration camp.

Death stared her in the face every day during those years. Yet in the mist of unspeakable horror and agony, she held secret Bible studies and taught fellow inmates how to face life and death with Jesus Christ. Corrie once said, "I have experienced His presence in the deepest hell that man can create. I have really tested the promises of the Bible, and believe me, you can count on them."

She also knew the extreme importance of memorizing the Scriptures. She stated, "Gather the riches of God's promises. Nobody can take away from you those texts from the Bible which you have learned by heart."[2]

Corrie knew that while evil men could take much of earth's pleasures (and even necessities) from her, they could not take away the promises of God that she had long committed to heart. In God's providence, Corrie ten Boom was set free; and in the years to come, God opened a worldwide ministry for her—a ministry that was, no doubt, made all the more meaningful because of the suffering she had experienced. "The stronger the winds, the deeper the roots, and the longer the winds…the more beautiful the tree."[3] Truly, the precious promises of God yielded much fruit in the life and ministry of Corrie ten Boom. They will yield much fruit in ours as well if we will believe and claim them.

Thus, it is in the Word of God that his very character is described (what he is like), and we grow in our understanding of what he is like by meditating on his attributes and his promises.

Having considered some of the attributes of God in the last chapter, let's now look at some of his promises. The apostle Peter says that God "has granted to us his precious and very great promises" (2 Peter 1:4). That says a lot about the promises of God. Indeed, they would be too good to be true if made by anyone but God. However, they *are* made by him and, therefore, cannot fail. This is all the more reason for us to give continual attention to his extraordinary promises, especially during the times in which we live.

So how do the promises of God help us know what he is like? How do they help us live in a very wicked and confused culture? Read carefully the instructive and encouraging words of Puritan writer Samuel Clark:

> A fixed, constant attention to the promises,
> and a firm belief of them, would prevent solici-
> tude and anxiety about the concerns of this life.

> It would keep the mind quiet and composed in every change, and support and keep up our sinking spirits under the several troubles of life... Christians deprive themselves of their most solid comforts by their unbelief and forgetfulness of God's promises. For there is no extremity so great, but there are promises suitable to it, and abundantly sufficient for our relief in it.[4]

Wise words. The promises of God "keep the mind quiet and composed in every change." This is true in our day of *enormous* change, as well as at any other time in history. Furthermore, it will continue to be true as long as we live.

Therefore, let us remember that God's promises help us better know what he is like, as well as equipping us to face our culture with confidence and to have a godly impact upon it. Let's look then at some of God's magnificent promises to his people.

God Promises Us His *Presence*

The presence of God with his people is an immensely encouraging theme throughout Scripture. For example, as Moses was leading the people toward the promised land, God said to him in Exodus 33:14, "My presence will go with you, and I will give you rest."

In later years, God said to Joshua, "Do not be frightened, and do not be dismayed, for the Lord your God is with you wherever you go" (Joshua 1:9). In Isaiah 41:10, the Lord declares, "Fear not, for I am with you; be not dismayed, for I am your God; I will strengthen you, I will help you, I will uphold you with my righteous right hand."

When the apostle Paul was being opposed in Acts 18, God said to him one night in a vision, "Do not be afraid, but go on speaking and do not be silent, for I am with you" (Acts 18:18:9–10). What an amazing encouragement there is in the promise of God's presence with his people!

Furthermore, recall that Jesus said to his disciples, "I am with you always, to the end of the age" (Matthew 28:20). It is significant that Matthew ends his Gospel account with these words of Jesus for at the beginning of his book, he quotes Isaiah 7:14 with its prediction of the coming Messiah, whose name is *Immanuel*, a title that means "God with us."

We should also note the phrase "to the end of the age," which means that Jesus is with us until he returns to establish his earthy kingdom. The Bible teaches us that he is the same yesterday, today, and tomorrow. So he is with his people today just as much as in previous generations—a glorious fact that should bring continual joy to our hearts.

Let us then give fervent thanksgiving for the promise of God's presence. Let us also determine to *practice* his presence through daily meditation on his Word and constant communion with him in prayer and praise.

The seventeenth-century French monk Nicholas Hermann (known as Brother Lawrence) passionately emphasized the practice of God's presence and wrote, "There is not in the world a kind of life more sweet and delightful than that of a continual conversation with God… Were I a preacher, I should, above all other things, preach the practice of the presence of God."[5]

> Be thou my Vision, O Lord of my heart;
> Naught be all else to me, save that thou art.
> Thou my best thought, by day or by night,
> Waking or sleeping, thy presence my light.[6]

God Promises to *Keep* Us

The words of Jesus in John 10 continue to bring immense encouragement to believers the world over: "My sheep hear my voice, and I know them, and they follow me. I give them eternal life, and they will never perish, and no one will snatch them out of my hand" (John 10:27–28). Augustus Toplady expressed beautifully the joy of eternal security:

> My name from the palms of his hands
> Eternity will not erase;

impressed on his heart it remains,
in marks of indelible grace.
Yes, I to the end shall endure,
as sure as the earnest is given;
more happy, but not more secure,
the glorified spirits in heaven![7]

Yes, we are secure for eternity, but God also has purposes for us in *this* life. For example, Paul says, "And I am sure of this, that he who began a good work in you will bring it to completion at the day of Jesus Christ" (Philippians 1:6).

Throughout our lives, God works in and through us—often in unseen ways. We may not always see the evidence of his work as we would desire, but his work is taking place nonetheless. Moreover, because we belong to him, we can trust God for his protection throughout this life. David prays in Psalm 32:7, "You are a hiding place for me; you preserve me from trouble; you surround me with shouts of deliverance." Furthermore, be encouraged by David's great song of deliverance in 2 Samuel 22:

> This God—his way is perfect; the word of
> the Lord proves true; he is a shield for all those who
> take refuge in him. For who is God, but the Lord?
> And who is a rock, except our God? This God is
> my strong refuge and has made my way blameless.
> He made my feet like the feet of a deer and set me
> secure on the heights. (2 Samuel 22:31–34)

Yes, our complete security is in the Lord himself. As an unknown author has written: "Plagues and deaths around me fly; till He pleases, I cannot die." In his 1939 Christmas Day broadcast, with Great Britain at war, King George VI quoted lines from Minnie Haskins's poem of 1908 "God Knows":

> I said to the man who stood at the Gate of
> the Year, "Give me a light that I may tread safely

into the unknown." And he replied, "Go out into the darkness, and put your hand into the hand of God. That shall be to you better than light, and safer than a known way."[8]

We are living in days of great cultural darkness, even to an extent we have never before seen in our lifetimes. However, regardless of our society's foolish and self-destructive worldview, resulting in constant assaults on biblical truth and values, we have that which is far better than a familiar and known way; we have the hand of God to guide and keep us.

> How firm a foundation, ye saints of the Lord,
> Is laid for your faith in His excellent Word!
> What more can He say than to you He hath said,
> To you who for refuge to Jesus have fled?

> "The soul that on Jesus hath leaned for repose
> I will not, I will not desert to his foes;
> That soul, though all hell should endeavor to
>   shake,
> I'll never, no never, no never forsake!"[9]

David prayed, "You make known to me the path of life; in your presence there is fullness of joy; at your right hand are pleasures forevermore" (Psalm 16:11). Always remember that a deteriorating culture cannot change this exhilarating truth: all who belong to God and are led by him rejoice greatly in his continual presence!

Indeed, our times are in God's hands (Psalm 31:15), and we can trust him to protect us and use us. Therefore, when we see religious liberty and freedom of speech coming under attack in our nation and hostile governments growing in power and influence, we can turn to the promise of God's presence and find perspective, encouragement, strength, and freedom from fear.

Mark Twain is reported to have quipped, "I've known a great many troubles in my life, most of which never happened." That's good to remember when we are tempted to worry about the future, but it's even better to read and reflect on the words of Jesus in Matthew 6:25–34. In verse 26, he says, "Look at the birds of the air: they neither sow nor reap nor gather into barns, and yet your heavenly Father feeds them. Are you not of more value than they?"

The Bible teaches that by God's power, we are being "guarded ("kept" in NKJV) through faith for a salvation ready to be revealed in the last time" (1 Peter 1:5).

Kept by God!

For time and eternity.

The very nature of eternal life itself.

What could possibly bring greater confidence, joy, and security?

God Promises to *Guide* Us

This is a wonderfully encouraging promise for all of us need guidance from God. We need it every day. The Bible says, "Who is the man who fears the Lord? Him will he instruct in the way that he should choose" (Psalm 25:12). In Psalm 32:8, God says, "I will instruct you and teach you in the way you should go; I will counsel you with my eye upon you."

Thus, because God is perfect, his guidance is perfect—a guidance that is always for his glory and for our good. Therefore, we can rejoice in it even though it is often not exactly what we expected. For example, think about the Israelites as they traveled in the wilderness toward the promised land. They had no clue it would take forty years to get there! How many times do you suppose Moses heard the question "Are we there yet?"

However, in leading the Israelites as he did, God wanted to give them something far greater than a piece of real estate. He was offering them an opportunity to know him in his greatness and power. Consequently, his plan would take them *the longer way around* so that they would learn to know and trust God in every circumstance they faced on the journey. As Thomas Brooks put it, "God hath in Himself all power to defend you...all grace to enrich you...all goodness to supply you."[10]

Moreover, the reality is that God often sends *us* the longer way around. Why? It is because he sees things we cannot see. He knows the road we should take even though it appears to us to be an unwanted, unnecessary, longer way.

King David went the longer way to the throne—and he didn't get there without some detours. Paul went the longer way to Rome. Thus, we must recognize that the shortest way is not the best way if it is not God's way. This is true because he knows exactly what he's doing as he works all things according to his perfect desires. Thus, he obviously doesn't take us the longer way around to wear us out or confuse us. To the contrary, he does it because he loves us, sees what we don't see, and has purposes for our lives that will be revealed in the course of the journey. Thank God for his promise to guide us.

Furthermore, we should not just seek God's guidance; we should also seek God himself—something that is supremely important and must be done above all else. In other words, don't just seek something *from* him. Seek *him*!

Certainly, we should ask for his guidance and trust him for it, but beyond all else, let us seek the Lord for who he is in himself.

God Promises to *Provide* for Us

The Bible says of Abraham that he was "fully convinced that God was able to do what he had promised" (Romans 4:21). Furthermore, down through the centuries, God has faithfully kept his promise to provide for his people.

For example, the great missionary Hudson Taylor was one who knew that God was able to do what he had promised. So he went into a bank in Brighton, England, to open a bank account for the China Inland Mission. On the application, he was asked to indicate his assets, so he wrote, "Ten pounds and the promises of God."[11]

I don't know what the banker thought of that response, but Hudson Taylor knew he could count on the promise of God to provide for the missionary endeavors to which he had been called. We, too, can know and rejoice in God's promise to provide; in fact, all through Scripture, we see this highly encouraging truth clearly proclaimed.

> I have been young, and now am old, yet I have not seen the righteous forsaken or his children begging for bread. (Psalm 37:25)

> Humble yourselves, therefore, under the mighty hand of God so that at the proper time he may exalt you, casting all your anxieties on him, because he cares for you. (1 Peter 5:6–7)

> And my God will supply every need of yours according to his riches in glory in Christ Jesus. (Philippians 4:19)

God probably won't answer all our questions, but he has certainly promised to meet all our needs. Furthermore, he often does it in unexpected ways using unexpected people.

The story is told of an elderly lady who once had no money to buy food. She prayed, "Dear Lord, please send me a side of bacon and a sack of corn meal." Over and over, she prayed this prayer aloud (a very specific one, I might add).

Eventually, one of the town's unscrupulous individuals decided to play a trick on her by dropping a side of bacon and a sack of corn meal down her chimney. It landed right in front of her as she knelt in prayer.

Jumping to her feet, she exclaimed, "Oh, Lord, you've answered my prayer!" Then she went all over town telling everyone her good news.

Now this was too much for the impish prankster who dropped the food down her chimney. He ridiculed her publicly and told her that God didn't answer her prayer...*he* did.

The lady replied, "Well, the devil may have *brought* it, but it was the Lord who *sent* it!"

It is true that God constantly reverses the plans of Satan by bringing good out of evil and accomplishing his divine purposes (see

Genesis 50:20). Thank God for his daily provision for us whatever our need may be—whether spiritual, physical, emotional, relational, or financial ("every need of yours," Philippians 4:19). Truly, the believer has an inheritance that can never be lost, resources that can never be depleted, and a life that can never die.

> Fear not! I am with thee; O be not dismayed,
> For I am thy God, and will still give thee aid;
> I'll strengthen thee, help thee, and cause thee to
>   stand,
> Upheld by My righteous, omnipotent hand.[12]

God Promises to *Strengthen* Us

We have the promise that God "gives power to the faint, and to him who has no might he increases strength" (Isaiah 40:29). Isaiah 40:31 says, "They who wait for the Lord shall renew their strength." The word *renew* points to a boundless supply of fresh strength. This strength, of course, comes from God for the word *renew* means *to exchange*. That is to say, we exchange our strength for God's strength. Had you rather have the strength of God or the strength of man? We don't have to think long and hard about that one!

Then as we see in verse 31, those with this renewed strength "shall mount up with wings like eagles." The reason these majestic birds provide the perfect analogy for this context is because the time comes when the molting eagle exchanges its old feathers for new ones and, as a result, can fly to phenomenal heights.

Likewise, those who wait for the Lord exchange *their* strength for *his* strength and, as a result, mount up with wings like eagles. However, we must make sure we are truly waiting for the Lord, which means setting our hope on him with fervent longing and believing him to fulfill his promises. Raymond Ortlund Jr. has written:

> It will not do to put my faith in God while I keep my heart on this world. God will not under-write my worldliness with his power. He never

promised the soaring strength of eagles so I could
go on grunting in the sty of Babylon.[13]

Isaiah 40:31 goes on to say: "They shall run and not be weary; they shall walk and not faint." We all face times when we desperately need to exchange our strength for God's strength—seasons of weakness, weariness, and uncertainty. Such predicaments can seem impossible to navigate or resolve.

For example, in the Old Testament, King Jehoshaphat certainly faced an impossible situation—an ominous enemy threatening the land of Judah. So the king prayed: "O our God, will you not execute judgment on them? For we are powerless against this great horde that is coming against us. We do not know what to do, but our eyes are on you" (2 Chronicles 20:12).

That's what God wanted to hear! He then communicated this message to Jehoshaphat and the people by saying, "Thus says the Lord to you, Do not be afraid and do not be dismayed at this great horde, for the battle is not yours but God's" (2 Chronicles 20:15). Needless to say, the enemy never had a chance!

This story is an example of *exchanged* strength: the strength of man (which was totally inadequate, to say the least) was exchanged for the strength of God (which is always adequate for every situation of life).

Therefore, whatever you face, you can say to the Lord, "My eyes are on you." Then as we wait for him, we trust him to provide all the strength, all the direction, and all the provision we need. The apostle Paul declares, "I can do all things through him who strengthens me" (Philippians 4:13). Always remember that God's strength is perfect strength, adequate strength, supernatural strength, and available strength—ours to claim.

Thus, "we'll never awaken to a morning in which the Lord has given us work to do or burdens to bear without providing the strength we need."[14] So even in the midst of our culture's moral insanity, we can rejoice in the fact that because our life is *in* Christ and our strength is *from* him, we can do all things *through* him and thus bring glory *to* him.

Therefore, depend on the Lord alone for every daily need of your life, knowing that he who "upholds the universe by the word of his power" (Hebrews 1:3) will uphold you with his strength.

> Day by day and with each passing moment,
> Strength I find to meet my trials here;
> Trusting in my Father's wise bestowment,
> I've no cause for worry or for fear.[15]

God Promises to Give Us *Wisdom*

Wisdom from God is important in any age, and our age is certainly no exception. Clearly, our own knowledge and wisdom seem very inadequate when so many things in this rapidly changing world are spiraling out of control. Sooner or later, it becomes obvious that academic, material, and technological advances do not automatically result in wisdom. As someone quipped, it may be a smartphone, but it is not a *wise* phone.

The good news, however, is that wisdom is available—not the fading wisdom of this world but the true wisdom of God. It is a wisdom that, as Proverbs 3:15 declares, is "more precious than jewels, and nothing you desire can compare with her."

While this wisdom can propel us forward on the most perplexing of days, it is a wisdom that is at odds with much of the ideology of today's culture. This is because biblical positions on issues like integrity, morality, sexual identity, and the sacredness of human life (born and unborn) are simply dismissed as antiquated concepts. Furthermore, standing firm on such positions can be vastly unpopular and quite costly. However, some things are worth the cost!

Therefore, without question, God's wisdom is absolutely critical in the cultural confusion so evident in our day. So how do we obtain wisdom? According to Proverbs 2, we must *seek* it.

> If you call out for insight and raise your
> voice for understanding, if you seek it like silver
> and search for it as for hidden treasures, then you

will understand the fear of the Lord and find the knowledge of God. For the Lord gives wisdom; from his mouth come knowledge and under-standing. (Proverbs 2:3–6)

Thus, we don't get wisdom automatically. We must seek it and call out to God for it. James 1:5 says, "If any of you lacks wisdom, let him ask God, who gives generously to all without reproach, *and it will be given him*" (emphasis mine). This is God's promise—and what a marvelous promise it is! However, we must make sure that we *ask* for this wisdom, and, as James goes on to say, we must "ask in faith, with no doubting" (James 1:6).

In Psalm 119:130, we see how God gives us his wisdom: "The unfolding of your words gives light; it imparts understanding to the simple." So we gain wisdom from God through his Word. Hence, we must daily immerse ourselves in reading, studying, and meditating upon the Scriptures. To do so is to avail ourselves of "the wisdom from above" (James 3:17).

Furthermore, God's wisdom guards us. See if you think the next few verses in Proverbs 2 sound like our culture today. The biblical writer is speaking here of wisdom, knowledge, and discretion guarding us.

It will rescue you from the way of evil—from anyone who says perverse things, from those who abandon the right paths to walk in ways of darkness, from those who enjoy doing evil and celebrate perversion, whose paths are crooked, and whose ways are devious. (Proverbs 2:12–15 CSB)

Thus, wisdom protects us from the way of evil, from those of perverted speech, and, as we see in Proverbs 2:16–19, from sexual impurity. Our society today seems filled with these elements.

Many politicians don't operate with true wisdom.

Educators don't always display wisdom.

Corporate America often fails to exhibit wisdom.

However, God's people *can* know wisdom—*his* wisdom.

Therefore, rejoice in this promise and seek the wisdom of God by diligently pursuing him through his Word and fervently asking him for guidance, understanding, and the power to apply his wisdom in your life.

God Promises to Do *Good* for Us

Because God is good—perfectly good—he does good for his people. The nature of this goodness is seen in Jeremiah 32:40–41 where he says to the people of Israel: "I will make with them an everlasting covenant, that *I will not turn away from doing good to them.* And I will put the fear of me in their hearts, that they may not turn from me. *I will rejoice in doing them good* and I will plant them in this land in faithfulness, with all my heart and all my soul" (emphasis mine).

In Psalm 84:11, the psalmist says, "For the Lord God is a sun and shield; the Lord bestows favor and honor. No good thing does he withhold from those who walk uprightly."

In the Old Testament, Joseph said to his brothers (who had so mistreated him years earlier), "As for you, you meant evil against me, but God meant it for *good*, to bring it about that many people should be kept alive, as they are today" (Genesis 50:20, emphasis mine).

Clearly, Joseph understood something of the providence of God. He had learned that God overrules the worst that humans can do, and because he is all-powerful, he can bring good out of evil. F. W. Faber puts this spiritual principle in poetic form:

> Ill that He blesses is our good,
> and unblest good is ill;
> and all is right that seems most wrong,
> if it be His sweet will.

Thus, it is a joy to know that before any crisis comes our way, God has already made a more than sufficient provision to meet it.

That provision is always timed perfectly, as we see in the remarkable story of Joseph.

One of the most familiar verses in the New Testament is Romans 8:28: "And we know that for those who love God all things work together for good, for those who are called according to his purpose." Charles Spurgeon referred to this truth as the best promise of this life:

> Everything that happens to you is for your own good. If the waves roll against you, it only speeds your ship toward the port. If lightning and thunder come, the rain clears the atmosphere and promotes your soul's health. You gain by loss, you grow healthy in sickness, you live by dying, and you are made rich in losses.
>
> Could you ask for a better promise? It is better that all things should work for my good than all things should be as I would wish to have them. All things might work for my pleasure and yet might all work my ruin. If all things do not always please me, they will always benefit me.
>
> This is the best promise of this life.[16]

Yes, in his guidance, God may take us the longer way around (as mentioned earlier) and use trials and challenges in our lives. However, he orders every step of the journey to teach us and to grow us. Most of all, he uses the circumstances and events of our lives to point us to Jesus—the one who came that we might have eternal and abundant life.

God has fulfilled his promise again and again to do good for us. He will continue to do so.

> Blessed be the God and Father of our Lord Jesus Christ, who has blessed us in Christ with every spiritual blessing in the heavenly places, even as he chose us in him before the foundation

of the world, that we should be holy and blameless before him. In love he predestined us for adoption as sons through Jesus Christ, according to the purpose of his will. (Ephesians 1:3–5)

If Paul looks into the *past* before the creation of the world, he sees that God foreknew and predestined his people to be conformed to the image of Christ. Moreover, if Paul looks into the *recent* past, he sees that God called and justified his people whom he had predestined. Then if Paul looks toward the *future* when Jesus returns, he sees that God has determined to gather his people to himself that they might fellowship and reign with him for all eternity in perfect, glorified bodies. Think about that reality. From eternity to eternity, God has acted with the good of his people in mind. What a stunning and encouraging truth to continually ponder!

Furthermore, we should remember that God not only *does* good for us, he *is* our good. "Oh, taste and see that the Lord is good! Blessed is the man who takes refuge in him!" (Psalm 34:8, see also 100:5).

The great theologian Jonathan Edwards preached the magnificent truth of God's goodness by declaring that believers have all their objective good in him. Edwards said:

> God himself is the great good which they are brought to the possession and enjoyment of by redemption. He is the highest good, and the sum of all that good which Christ purchased. God is the inheritance of the saints; he is the portion of their souls. God is their wealth and treasure, their food, their life, their dwelling place, their ornament and diadem, and their everlasting honor and glory. They have none in heaven but God; he is the great good which the redeemed are received to at death, and which they are to rise to at the end of the world.[17]

Moreover, if God has always acted for our good, and will continue to do so in the future, will he not also in our present circumstances work everything together for his glory and our good? Indeed, he will. It's his promise. He does good for his people (see Romans 8:32).

Furthermore, because this gracious God inhabits his people through the Holy Spirit, believers are empowered to reflect God's goodness in the way they live and in the service they render to him and to others. "Trust in the Lord, and do what is good; dwell in the land and live securely" (Psalm 37:3 CSB).

God Promises Us His *Peace*

This promise is especially meaningful, living as we do in a world that knows little peace, for it is a world of enormous spiritual darkness—a darkness reflected in moral confusion and various forms of violence and abuse such as shootings, suicides, terrorism, rape, and sex trafficking.

However, there is welcome comfort for believers even in the midst of such a tumultuous and decadent world. Jesus says:

> Peace I leave with you; my peace I give to you. Not as the world gives do I give to you. Let not your hearts be troubled, neither let them be afraid... I have said these things to you, that in me you may have peace. In the world you will have tribulation. But take heart; I have overcome the world. (John 14:27, 16:33)

> Yes, 'tis sweet to trust in Jesus,
> Just from sin and self to cease;
> Just from Jesus simply taking
> Life and rest, and joy and peace.[18]

In the midst of our nation's cultural insanity, is it truly possible to receive from Jesus *life and rest and joy and peace*? Indeed, it is!

Our all-powerful Savior and Lord is able to provide exactly what his people need—even in the most perilous of times. Charles Swindoll has written: "When will we ever learn that there are no hopeless situations, only people who have grown hopeless about them?"[19]

Let us then refuse to grow hopeless and instead grow in the all-sufficient grace of God and live daily in the supernatural life and peace he provides. The apostle Paul gives us the key to this kind of victorious living when he says:

> Do not be anxious about anything, but in everything by prayer and supplication with thanksgiving let your requests be made known to God. And the peace of God, which surpasses all understanding, will guard your hearts and your minds in Christ Jesus. (Philippians 4:6–7)

The word *guard* in this verse is a military term, and it is one of the strongest terms used in the New Testament. It means *preserve, keep,* or *to keep under guard as a garrison.*

Also, it is worth noting that Paul was writing these words to believers who lived in the city of Philippi, a city that was a Roman colony with a military garrison. So the believers there would have picked up on Paul's analogy, understanding that it is not Roman soldiers who guarded them but rather the peace of God himself.

Perhaps the Roman Christians called to mind the prayer of the prophet Isaiah, "You keep him in perfect peace whose mind is stayed on you, because he trusts in you" (Isaiah 26:3). Think of it: kept in God's perfect peace! So who or what can successfully come against those whom God protects? (See Romans 8:31.)

Furthermore, Paul's use of a military term in Philippians 4:7 implies that the mind is in a battle zone and needs to be protected. God's peace truly provides this impenetrable defense, and in this, we can continually rejoice.

Furthermore, Paul wrote, "But the Lord is faithful. He will establish you and guard you against the evil one" (2 Thessalonians 3:3). What a great promise! Since God can guard us against the devil, as this verse declares, he can guard us against anything that would threaten our lives and ministries.

We have surely seen quite a number of various threats in recent years: the advances of radical ideologies, massive political and social unrest, natural disasters, a global pandemic, violence throughout the cities of America, and far-reaching governmental corruption.

Furthermore, it appears that religious persecution is coming (if not already here in some forms). So how do we respond in the midst of a hostile culture? How do we respond when circumstances in our own lives are threatening our security and peace? Elisabeth Elliot gives a wonderfully insightful and practical word at this point:

> On dark days when the only song we feel
> like singing is a dirge, we can pray, "Let the music
> of thy promises be on my tongue" (Ps. 119:172).
> This is no tear-jerking ballad of how I'm feeling.
> The promises of God will lift me right out of sad
> sentimentality and put music in my mouth if I
> will think steadily on them.[20]

Therefore, regardless of your feelings, determine to confess and sing the truth of God's eternal Word. Nothing is as spiritually refreshing as the peace God gives us as we constantly engage the Scriptures with a heart of faith.

> The peace of Christ makes fresh my heart,
> A fountain ever springing!
> All things are mine since I am His—
> How can I keep from singing?
> No storm can shake my inmost calm
> while to that Rock I'm clinging.
> Since Christ is Lord of Heaven and earth,
> how can I keep from singing?[21]

It is an indescribable joy and comfort to know that our lives and ministries are in the hands of God and that we can trust him to give us courage, strength, and a continual peace that surpasses all understanding. Church history certainly bears out the reality of God's perfect peace being given to his children throughout the generations.

For example, the great preacher Savonarola of Florence, Italy (1452–1498), was persecuted for his faith and preaching and was eventually executed. However, before his death, he said this: "He who believes that Christ rules above, need not fear what happens below."[22] Yes, the key to peace is trusting in the sovereign Lord who gives it.

Therefore, may we heed Paul's exhortation every day, "And let the peace of Christ rule in your hearts, to which indeed you were called in one body. And be thankful" (Colossians 3:15). Hence, we can appreciate the prayer of F. B. Meyer (and make it our own):

> I humbly ask, O Christ, that your peace
> may be the garrison of my heart, with its affections, and of my mind, with its thoughts. May
> your peace reign in me and out of this peace may
> I serve.[23]

God Promises to Make All Things *New*

An inscription on the Capitol dome in Washington, DC, says: "One God, one law, one element, and one supreme event toward which the whole creation moves."[24] Although the inscription does not identify it, students of the Bible know that the one supreme event toward which all of history is moving is the return of the Lord Jesus Christ. As the apostle John declares, "We know that when he appears we shall be like him, because we shall see him as he is" (1 John 3:2).

> But, oh! No foe invades the bliss,
> When glory crowns the Christian's head,
> One view of Jesus as he is
> Will strike all sin forever dead.[25]

Furthermore, the apostle John says:

> Then I saw a new heaven and a new earth, for the first heaven and the first earth had passed away... And he who was seated on the throne said, "Behold, I am making all things new." (Revelation 21:1, 5)

In that coming day, God will create a new universe for those who know Christ, where they will live and reign with him forever. To that end, Vance Havner has written:

> I have thought that if this world, marred and spoiled by sin, can be so lovely, what will the new earth be like when God has freed it from dictators, disease, death, and the devil and filled it with His glory as the waters cover the sea.[26]

Over the years, some of the finest Bible teachers have differed on their millennial views and the framework for Christ's return. However, the great theologian Augustine spoke to the heart of the matter in a very helpful way:

> He who loves the coming of the Lord is not he who affirms that it is far off, nor is it he who says it is near, but rather he who, whether it be far off or near, awaits it with sincere faith, steadfast hope, and fervent love.[27]

In the new day that's coming, everything wrong will be put right and every tear will be wiped away (Revelation 21:3–4). The promise of God is that we will live forever, reign with Christ forever, and be forever free from sin, sorrow, and death. Oh, what an indescribable day that is coming!

Yet we still live in *this* day, one that is becoming more and more challenging due to the culture's unbiblical, and even antibiblical, worldview. No doubt, this is why people will sometimes ask in dismay, "What is this world coming to?" Well, you could answer that question this way: "Here's what it is coming to. At the name of Jesus, every knee will bow 'in heaven and on earth and under the earth, and every tongue confess that Jesus Christ is Lord, to the glory of God the Father' (Philippians 2:10–11). That's what this world is coming to!" Thus, you would be completely right in stating it that way because it is the absolute truth of God's Word!

Yes, this world is coming to the point of total subjection to Jesus Christ and to the full acknowledgment of his sovereign authority! Of course, this does not mean that everyone will be saved (as universalism teaches), but it does mean that everyone will ultimately realize that Jesus is Lord after all!

Hence, what does this mean for us right now? It means that if a day is coming when we will acknowledge Christ as Lord, we should also want to do it now. If there is going to be a time when every tongue will confess Jesus Christ as Lord, we should also want to practice that now. Therefore, let's be and do *now* what we are going to be and do *then*. For our supreme, sovereign, resurrected, and exalted Lord is worthy of our purest devotion and highest praise!

Moreover, as a result of Christ's victory over death and the devil, God has given us his glorious promise that one day he will make all things new!

> Battle won.
> War over.
> Victory complete.
> Suffering fulfilled.
> Woes accomplished.
> Promises kept.
> Lovers faithful.
> Joy eternal.
> Hope realized.
> Faith sight.
> Kingdom come.
> Name hallowed.[28]

The absolute certainty of our future in Christ should be a constant source of inexpressible joy, no matter the shocking changes and chaotic developments in our culture and world. Randy Alcorn has stated:

> Someday this upside-down world will be turned right side up. Nothing in all eternity will turn it back again. If we are wise, we will spend our brief lives on earth positioning ourselves for the turn.[29]

Yes, our lives on this earth are brief (James 4:14), and we should make every day count as we eagerly anticipate our returning Christ who will make all things new.

Someone quipped, "I intend to live forever. So far, so good." Humorous optimism, to be sure. However, eternal life is not based on optimism; neither is it contingent on physical life. For believers, it is dependent on the very promise of Jesus himself who said, "Truly, truly, I say to you, whoever hears my word and believes him who sent me has eternal life. He does not come into judgment, but has passed from death to life" (John 5:24).

Those who know and believe the words of Jesus and the One who sent him are promised eternal life—a life that begins the moment they come to faith in Christ (2 Corinthians 5:17). Thus, as believers, we rejoice that our most important citizenship is in heaven (Philippians 3:20). C. S. Lewis put it like this:

> If I find in myself a desire which no experience in this world can satisfy, the most probable explanation is that I was made for another world... I must keep alive in myself the desire for my true country, which I shall not find till after death.[30]

Made for another world—indeed. Regardless of what we face this side of heaven, we find great joy in the promise of God that he will one day make all things new. The apostle Paul says, "For I consider that the sufferings of this present time are not worth comparing with the glory that is to be revealed to us" (Romans 8:18).

The Puritan Samuel Rutherford surely had it right when he said, "Our little time of suffering is not worthy of our first night's welcome home to heaven." With our finite understanding, there may be much we cannot know about heaven, but the words of the seventeenth-century Puritan pastor Richard Baxter give us an encouraging reminder of the most important fact of all:

> My knowledge of that life is small.
> The eye of faith is dim.
> But 'tis enough that Christ knows all,
> And I shall be with him.[31]

Welsh pastor Peter Jeffery tells of a town in North Wales by the name of Bala. The language spoken in the homes and shops there is Welsh, and—with few exceptions—the names on the houses are Welsh. One of these exceptions is seen in the nameplate on a certain house, *Pros Kairon*. This name is Greek, not Welsh; the words mean *for a while*.

> It seems that whoever gave that name to his house had an understanding of spiritual realities. He knew that no home is permanent on this earth; the house may stand for a hundred years or more, but people are here only *for a while*.[32]

Yes, life for us in this world is temporary. However, as beings who are made in the image of God with immortal souls, we rejoice in the life God has given us through his Son—life that is *eternal* (1 John 5:13)!

I am certainly thankful for the roof over my head, and I love the state and nation in which I live, but this earth is not my final home. I'm only here "for a while." Jesus says, "If I go and prepare a place for you, I will come again and will take you to myself, that where I am you may be also" (John 14:3).

Yes, God has promised to make all things new.

End of story.

Yet...the end is only the beginning.

It surely makes us want to say with the apostle John, "Come, Lord Jesus!" (Revelation 22:20). Therefore, until that glorious day arrives, let us simply say...*Pros Kairon*!

There are, of course, many more gracious promises of God besides the ones we've considered in this chapter (e.g., God promises to forgive confessed sin, answer prayer, fulfill prophecy, and build his church). However, I believe the promises we have considered will show that *all* of God's promises to his people are true and will bring encouragement to their heart and renewal to their spirit.

Think about it like this. Have you ever really wanted something to happen, but you weren't sure it would, so you said, "I'm not getting my hopes up"? Perhaps you were concerned that a friend would be disappointed if he didn't get the particular news he wanted, so you said, "Now don't get your hopes up."

However, when it comes to the promises of God, he says in essence, "Get your hopes up!" That's because our hope is in *him*—an absolutely never failing, unshakable hope made abundantly clear to us through God's Word.

We have hope for the present, for the future, and for eternity.

Thus, one of the most important things we can do during these days of change and uncertainty is to review and meditate on the "precious and very great promises of God" (2 Peter 1:4).

> For God is not unjust so as to overlook your work and the love that you have shown for his name in serving the saints, as you still do. And we desire each one of you to show the same earnestness to have the full assurance of hope until the end, so that you may not be sluggish, but imitators of those who through faith and patience

inherit the promises. (Hebrews 6:10–12, emphasis mine)

Always remember: God is fully *able* to do what he says he will do; furthermore, he *will* do what he says he will do. He is faithful to keep every promise he has ever made!

> Blessed be the Lord who has given rest to his people Israel, according to all that he promised. Not one word has failed of all his good promise, which he spoke by Moses his servant. (1 Kings 8:56)

Therefore, ask God to empower you to refuse and reject the promises of sin and Satan and instead to receive, rejoice in, and act upon the hope-filled, life-transforming promises of God. Thomas Manton (1620–1677) said this: "Faith is lean and ready to starve unless it be fed with continual meditation on the promises."[33]

Therefore, read and reread the promises of God. Ponder them. Rejoice in them. Give thanks for them. You'll find faith and hope growing.

> Praise the Lord! For He is glorious;
> Never shall His promise fail;
> God hath made His saints victorious;
> Sin and death shall not prevail.[34]

PART 3

Life's Supreme Pursuit
Seeking the Knowledge of God

CHAPTER 6

Correctly Fearing God

The great twentieth-century preacher Martyn Lloyd-Jones said that when you are traveling through a bog, you look for solid ground. On a number of levels, our nation finds itself in a great bog, and consequently, multitudes of people are desiring some kind of solid ground. Sadly, however, most of them search for that ground in all the wrong places.

True solid ground is found only in the knowledge of God, a fact the Bible shows us repeatedly. For example, the apostle Paul prayed unceasingly that the Colossian believers would be filled with the knowledge of God's will "in all spiritual wisdom and understanding, so as to walk in a manner worthy of the Lord, fully pleasing to him, bearing fruit in every good work and increasing in the knowledge of God" (Colossians 1:9–10).

Increasing in the knowledge of God—this is indeed life's supreme pursuit for "by learning, experiencing, and rejoicing in the knowledge of God, we receive the greatest of blessings and God receives the highest glory."[1]

Of course, it is those who have been sought and found by God who seek to know him more fully throughout all of life. John Stott has penned these words:

> You can never take God by surprise. You
> can never anticipate him. He always makes the

first move. He is always there "in the beginning."
Before man existed, God acted. Before man stirs
himself to seek God, God has sought man. In the
Bible we do not see man groping after God; we
see God reaching after man.[2]

Yes, it is God who seeks after us. For example, the story is told
of a man who was being examined for ordination to the ministry. He
was asked how he had become a Christian, to which he replied, "I did
my part and God did his."

Well, that didn't sound right, so the ordaining council asked
him to explain what he meant by *his* part in salvation. He replied,
"My part was to run from God as fast as I could. God's part was to
run after me and catch me and bring me into his family."

The man gave a perfectly biblical answer because all of us were
born running from God. If God had not taken the initiative to go
after us, we would *still* be running away from him. Once we are
sought and found, however, we have the great privilege and responsibility of seeking the Lord daily through his Word. "Let us give our
thoughts completely to knowing God," Brother Lawrence exhorts
us. "The more one knows him, the more one wants to know him."[3]

Thus says the Lord: "Let not the wise man
boast in his wisdom, let not the mighty man
boast in his might, let not the rich man boast in
his riches, but let him who boasts boast in this,
that he understands and knows me, that I am
the Lord who practices steadfast love, justice, and
righteousness in the earth. For in these things I
delight, declares the Lord." (Jeremiah 9:23–24)

What an indescribable privilege it is to understand and know
our sovereign Lord, to pursue the knowledge of him every day, and
to grow in his grace as a result. How crucial it is for believers to have
this kind of foundation for life as they face the massive cultural confusion of our age. In 1920, T. S. Eliot asked these questions: Where

is the life we have lost in living? Where is the wisdom we have lost in knowledge? Where is the knowledge we have lost in information?[4]

What would Eliot say about our vacuous culture today? We are deluged with information, but that is no guarantee of true life, wisdom, and knowledge. In fact, it seems we have a startling shortage of those qualities in our nation at present.

Furthermore, people today are so often urged to focus on themselves and their own desires. However, as John Piper has wisely said, "To make them feel good about themselves when they were made to feel good about seeing God is like taking someone to the Alps and locking them in a room full of mirrors."[5] Thus, it is only a knowledge of God and his ways that will provide the direction, fulfillment, and sense of purpose that is sadly missing from individuals who simply look within themselves for these things.

This is all the more reason to heed Hosea 6:3, "Let us know; let us press on to know the Lord." Moreover, the more we know God, the more we are able to reflect him to a culture that does *not* know him. Truly, our highest privilege is that of knowing our triune God and growing daily in that knowledge. In fact, we were created for this! We exist for him (1 Corinthians 8:6).

Indeed, this is at the heart of biblical theology for theology is not simply an intellectual discipline that gathers knowledge but rather the means whereby we grow in true godliness and devotion to our heavenly Father. According to theologian John D. Hannah, theology may be defined "as the distilled knowledge of God that is the foundation of a walk with God."[6] He goes on to elaborate:

> No one can walk with a person he or she does not know; neither can we say we walk with God if we do not have an accurate knowledge of Him. Theology is not about an admiration of a series of gathered insights, however wonderful these insights may be; it is about responding appropriately and regularly to God.[7]

Yet many people today (including many evangelicals) do not understand this vitally important reality. For example, in a previous church I pastored, a young lady spoke to me before the church service, saying, "You're not going to preach on doctrine or anything like that, are you?" Apparently, she had the idea that Bible doctrine is dry and dull.

On the contrary, there is nothing dull and dry about it! Just the opposite is true. Doctrine teaches us who God is, what he has done to redeem us, the amazing promises he's made in his Word, and the power he gives us for daily living. What could be more important and exciting than this?

Sadly, however, the failure to understand the significance of theology is not limited to the young. Seminary professor Charles Ryrie told the story of a board meeting of a well-known Christian institution where a speaker had emphasized the importance of preaching the Bible. He had brought a stirring message to the group, and about an hour later, one of the board members (who had heard the message) prayed that the institution would always preach the Bible and not be sidetracked onto "peripheral matters of doctrine and theology." As Charles Ryrie wrote: "An oxymoronic prayer, to say the least!"[8]

Unfortunately, many evangelicals would not have a problem with such a prayer. That's because they do not truly understand the meaning of the words *theology* and *doctrine* and how they relate to pursuing the knowledge of God. Many people would say, "Don't bother me with theology or doctrine, just give me some nice devotional thought from the Bible." But the truth is that if devotion is not based on correct doctrine, it's not going to be worth anything.

Thus, we can see why the apostle Paul wrote to believers, saying:

> I do not cease to give thanks for you, remembering you in my prayers, that the God of our Lord Jesus Christ, the Father of glory, may give you the Spirit of wisdom and of revelation in *the knowledge of him.* (Ephesians 1:17, emphasis mine)

Thus, having considered what the Bible says about the existence and character of God, we will now consider in this third section what Scripture says about the *knowledge* of God—that which we can call life's supreme pursuit. In fact, to pursue the knowledge of God is to pursue God himself.

Moreover, there are two biblical concepts that can help us better understand who God is, who we are, and what his purpose is for us on this earth. The first concept is the *fear of the Lord*, and the second one is *the image of God*. Thus, these are two key doctrines for every believer to understand and to be able to communicate to others. In this chapter, let's consider the first of these two vitally important truths.

There are, of course, many fears believers should *not* have; after all, consider how many times the Bible says "Fear not" or "Do not be afraid." However, there is one fear we *should* have—and that's the fear of the Lord for when we fear him, we have nothing else to fear!

Franklin Roosevelt famously said, "We have nothing to fear but fear itself." He was, no doubt, wanting to encourage a war-weary nation. However, his statement is not correct for the truth is that we have nothing to fear but *God* himself. Moreover, as Oswald Chambers put it, "The remarkable thing about fearing God is that, when you fear God, you fear nothing else; whereas, if you do not fear God, you fear everything else."

The prophet Isaiah asked, "Who among you fears the Lord?" (Isaiah 50:10). Truly, this is a critical question in our day for in an age of rampant relativism and self-centered humanistic ideology, we have to wonder how many people really understand and appreciate *the fear of the Lord*. Consequently, they will more often than not develop a wrong view of this biblical concept. Many people simply see God as inconsistent, like a human father who at times is helpful and encouraging to his children but at other times is abusive to them. On the other hand, they may view God as only a doting grandfather and forget that he is the eternal, infinite Creator. Thus, there is great need today for a true understanding of the nature of God and what our response should be to that knowledge.

Now obviously, there is a wrong kind of fear in Scripture, but the fear of the Lord is the right kind. Nevertheless, the question might be asked: Why does the Bible use the word *fear* in the phrase "the fear of the Lord"? The reason for this is because of God's majestic nature and awesome power, as we will consider presently.

What the Fear of the Lord *Means*

Let's note first, however, what this biblical truth does *not* mean. The fear of the Lord is, obviously, not a reference to *natural* fear. All of us, no doubt, have dealt with the emotion of fear in our lives. Living in a fallen and broken world as we do, there are many dangers that can cause us to fear.

Furthermore, there are, undoubtedly, many people these days who are saying, "I fear for our country." Thus, we can say that fear is something of a natural response.

Yet this kind of fear is not necessarily sinful fear. It seems that the emotion of fear is something that even Jesus felt in the garden of Gethsemane as he anticipated the horrors of the cross and being separated from his heavenly Father. Mark 14:33 says that Jesus was "greatly distressed and troubled." In fact, it was to the point where "his sweat became like great drops of blood falling down to the ground" (Luke 22:44).

Another kind of fear that is not meant by the fear of the Lord is *sinful* fear. Of course, this is a fear that Jesus never experienced since he was and is the sinless Son of God. Fear is sinful if it causes us to be afraid of God in the sense that we cower in his presence, as though he may strike us down at any moment. It's the kind of fear James tells us the demons have when they "believe—and shudder!" (James 2:19).

This is also the kind of fear Adam felt when he first sinned and then hid from God (Genesis 3:10). Thus, the nature of sinful fear is that it drives a person away from God rather than to him; it is certainly a goal of the devil to make people so afraid of God that they want to flee from him. However, as theologian Michael Reeves says, "The Spirit's work is the exact opposite: to produce in us a wonderful fear that wins and draws us *to* God."[9]

So what exactly does the fear of the Lord mean? Martin Luther helps us answer that question by giving an illustration of godly fear. First, there is the fear a prisoner has for his torturer. Second, there is the fear a son has who loves his father and does not want to offend him or let him down. This second kind of fear is that which can describe the fear of the Lord, and it results from considering his nature and his mighty works (Psalm 145:10–13). Stuart Briscoe put it like this:

> When we "fear the Lord," our overriding desire is to honor his majesty and respect his authority while appropriating his grace, reveling in his love, basking in his forgiveness, and seeking only to please him. And our deepest concern is that we do not besmirch his glory or dishonor his name. This is what it means to fear the Lord.[10]

Not surprisingly then, Scripture is replete with references to the fear of the Lord. For example, consider the following statements from the book of Psalms alone concerning this vitally important concept:

> Oh, how abundant is your goodness, which you have stored up for those who fear you. (Psalm 31:19)

> The steadfast love of the Lord is from everlasting to everlasting on those who fear him. (Psalm 103:17)

> The angel of the Lord encamps around those who fear him, and delivers them. (Psalm 34:7)

> The fear of the Lord is the beginning of wisdom; all those who practice it have a good understanding. (Psalm 111:10)

So the fear of the Lord is connected with receiving God's wisdom, knowing his goodness, experiencing his love, and having his deliverance. As theologian Kelly Kapic has written:

> Fearing the Lord means that we are not left to our own resources to control and survive the elements of creation, but that we can trust the Creator who sustains that creation, controls the future and has our best interests at heart (e.g., Prov. 23:17–18).[11]

God has revealed himself in his Word as all-wise, all-powerful, and perfectly holy, righteous, and good. Therefore, he must be held in utmost reverence so that the fear of the Lord becomes the absolute controlling motivation of the believer's life.

Thus, the fear of the Lord is to be embraced, not resisted or ignored; we are to fear him properly and take refuge in him continually. In doing so, we are empowered to speak and sing of his goodness and love with joy, praise, and thanksgiving.

Now in practical terms, how does the fear of the Lord affect us as believers? How *should* it affect us? How should it cause us to live on a daily basis?

What the Fear of the Lord *Requires*

First of all, this godly fear calls for a hatred of sin. Wisdom personified calls out, "The fear of the Lord is hatred of evil. Pride and arrogance and the way of evil and perverted speech I hate" (Proverbs 8:13). Furthermore, Scripture says that it is "by the fear of the Lord one turns away from evil" (Proverbs 16:6, see also 3:7). This is why Paul exhorts believers, saying, "Let us cleanse ourselves from every defilement of body and spirit, bringing holiness to completion in the fear of God" (2 Corinthians 7:1).

To truly know the fear of God is to know God himself. And in knowing him, we stand in awe of his majesty, power, and perfect holiness. Therefore, "if we treat our sin lightly, we demonstrate that we have no sense of the enormity of our offense against Almighty God."[12] Thus, sin is of the utmost seriousness for it is against God himself. Puritan theologian John Owen famously said, "Be killing sin or sin will be killing you." Moreover, it is the fear of the Lord that is the key to victorious living.

> The fear of the Lord is a fountain of life,
> that one may turn away from the snares of death.
> (Proverbs 14:27)

Secondly, the fear of the Lord requires that we receive his grace and forgiveness and walk daily in the freedom he provides. The psalmist prays, "But with you there is forgiveness, that you may be feared" (Psalm 130:4). Those who genuinely appreciate God's amazing forgiveness are those who truly understand and practice the fear of the Lord. As A. W. Tozer has said, "No one ever yet knew the true grace of God who had not first known the fear of God."[13]

Thus, there is no contradiction between the fear of the Lord and his glorious and awe-inspiring grace. As such it is an indescribable privilege to live every day in the knowledge of God's grace and in the joy of his forgiveness. This is true freedom, indeed!

> If you abide in my word, you are truly my
> disciples, and you will know the truth, and the
> truth will set you free. (John 8:31–32)

> For freedom Christ has set us free; stand
> firm therefore, and do not submit again to a yoke
> of slavery. (Galatians 5:1)

Thirdly, the fear of the Lord calls for the seeking of godly wisdom. In speaking of this wisdom, Proverbs 2:4–5 says: "If you seek it like silver and search for it as for hidden treasures, then you will understand the fear of the Lord and find the knowledge of God."

Moreover, the Bible teaches that in Christ "are hidden all the treasures of wisdom and knowledge" (Colossians 2:3). Therefore, coming to faith in Christ creates a thirst for true knowledge. This is why Jesus says, "Come to me, all who labor and are heavy-laden, and I will give you rest. Take my yoke upon you, and *learn* from me, for I am gentle and lowly in heart, and you will find rest for your souls" (Matthew 11:28–29, emphasis mine).

To learn from Jesus is to be discipled by him. That's what the word *learn* indicates in this verse. Have you been discipled by Jesus? Thus, our Lord is comparing the Christian life to a school in which he is to be both the subject matter and the teacher. We are to learn from him.

Furthermore, seeking the knowledge of God and growing in his wisdom is a pursuit that never ends. For when we fear God as we should, we will always long to know him more. Hence, this is not only the school into which every true believer has entered; it is also the one in which there is a *lifelong* course of study. It's the school from which we never graduate—at least not this side of heaven.

Therefore, we must never say (or even think), "I've finished my studies. I've learned enough about God…about Christ…about salvation…about grace…about the Christian life." No, of course not. So don't ever take your cap off and throw it in the air! We're still learning. And because Jesus is our teacher and leader, he gives us great joy and fulfillment in the learning and discipling process.

Therefore, who in his or her right mind would ever want to be finished with *this* school?

Fourthly, and supremely, the fear of the Lord requires fervent and continual worship on our part for he is infinitely worthy of such a response. Puritan writer William Secker said that a drop of praise is an unsuitable acknowledgment for an ocean of mercy.

David prays in Psalm 5:7, "But I, through the abundance of your steadfast love, will enter your house. I will bow down toward your holy temple in the fear of you." Here again we see love and fear placed side by side. Thus, David delighted in God's amazing love, which led him to stand in sheer awe of such a God, prompting his wholehearted praise.

The writer of Hebrews says, "Let us offer to God acceptable worship, with reverence and awe, for our God is a consuming fire"

(Hebrews 12:28). What then is acceptable worship? In Psalm 34:1–3, David reveals the characteristics of worship that pleases God. It is voluntary, constant, verbal, contagious, public, and boastful (in this case, the boasting is proper because the object is God himself).

Therefore, true worship has its focus—not on the act of worship itself but on the triune God: Father, Son, and Holy Spirit. Furthermore, heaven will be filled with eternal praise. In recording his vision of heaven, the apostle John wrote, "And from the throne came a voice saying, 'Praise our God, all you his servants, you who fear him, small and great'" (Revelation 19:5).

Thus, our unswerving focus on God himself is to be as true of corporate worship as it is of our private times of worship. C. S. Lewis said, "The perfect church service would be one we were almost unaware of; our attention would have been on God."

What the Fear of the Lord *Provides*

In Psalm 25:12–13, David presents three exciting truths related to the fear of the Lord. Before considering these, however, it is important to note how David approaches the Lord. He comes before him in genuine humility and brokenness; there's not a trace of arrogance, stubbornness, or haughtiness. David comes confessing his sin. In verse 11, he prays, "For your name's sake, O Lord, pardon my guilt, for it is great."

Therefore, it is only from a position of genuine humility and brokenness before the Lord that we can expect to experience the blessings of the next two verses. An unknown Puritan said, "If you can't come to God with a broken heart, come to him *for* a broken heart." Truly, the result of such brokenness will have a powerful effect on our children and the generations to come. Author Steven Lawson has written: "There is no one too weak for God to use—only people who are too strong in themselves."[14]

The fear of the Lord moves the focus from us to the Lord himself. At the same time, as we live in the fear of the Lord, we experience his gracious blessings being lavished upon us as we see in Psalm 25. Let's consider three of these.

First, the fear of the Lord provides spiritual direction. "Who is the man who fears the Lord? Him will he instruct in the way that he should choose" (Psalm 25:12). God says in Psalm 32:8, "I will instruct you and teach you in the way you should go; I will counsel you with my eye upon you."

The story is told about a traveler in Ireland who stopped and asked a man for directions. "My friend, if you were going to Dublin, which way would you go?"

The Irishman replied, "I wouldn't go there from here." Now that's a curious response!

Yet when you think about it, we obviously begin any journey by starting from where we are now. The same is true spiritually. We honestly recognize our current condition, seek the knowledge of God, and live in the fear of the Lord by accepting his Word and heeding his directions *now.*

Thus, our choices throughout life are to be based on God's instruction, and how blessed we are that he promises to provide that instruction! We don't just sail through life randomly. Our way is chosen by God himself, and we are to choose what he has *already* chosen.

> For we are his workmanship, created in Christ Jesus for good works, which God *prepared beforehand,* that we should walk in them. (Ephesians 2:10, emphasis mine)

Therefore, God doesn't simply say, "I've given you a brain, so *you* figure out my will for your life." No, the purpose of our mind is not that of leaning on our own understanding (see Proverbs 3:5–6) but rather that of seeking to encounter God by immersing ourselves in his Word. The result will be that of knowing *his* mind and *his* will, and on that basis, we are able to make wise decisions. This is why David prays, "Make me to know your ways, O Lord; teach me your paths" (Psalm 25:4).

Proverbs 1:7 says, "The fear of the Lord is the beginning of knowledge." Conversely, we can say that without that knowledge, our existence has no meaning and, even worse, eternity offers no hope.

The good news is that the wisdom and guidance we need from God are readily available, but we must respond to him in obedience and faith. For example, consider how God led Israel in the wilderness by means of the cloud of glory (Exodus 13:21). The Israelites could know that they were exactly in the will of God by simply looking toward the cloud. When it moved, they moved. When it stopped, they stopped. So the stops as well as the steps of God's people were daily directed by him.

The same is true for us, yet perhaps you're thinking, *Well, it sure would be nice to have a cloud to watch so that I could clearly know God's direction.* Actually, he has provided something better for us! He has given us his Word, and he has given us the indwelling Holy Spirit. Therefore, we can know God's will daily by being filled with the Spirit and saturated with the Word. God will lead us if we keep our eyes fixed on him.

Secondly, the fear of the Lord provides spiritual prosperity. "His soul shall abide in well-being" (Psalm 25:13). There are multitudes of people today who have *material* prosperity, but their souls are not abiding in *spiritual* prosperity. They gain what the world can give but miss what God can give. For example, in 1974, Marvin Hamlisch won three Academy Awards, but he said, "Three Oscars in my hands, and I come home and empty the cat litter. I had thought that success would make me happy, but it didn't."[15]

In sharp contrast to such accounts of famous yet disillusioned and unhappy people, King David experienced a spiritual prosperity and fulfillment only God himself could give him. He prayed:

> Remember me, O Lord, when you show favor to your people; help me when you save them, that I may look upon the prosperity of your chosen ones, that I may rejoice in the gladness of your nation, that I may glory with your inheritance. (Psalm 106:4–5)

What earthly treasure could possibly compare with the Lord's inheritance for his chosen ones? As believers, we may live in an entitlement-saturated culture, but we belong to an inheritance-saturated kingdom—an inheritance that is ours through Christ alone (see Romans 8:16–17; Ephesians 1:11–12, 18).

David also prayed, "Oh, guard my soul, and deliver me!" (Psalm 25:20). Throughout his life, David experienced God's presence, protection, and spiritual prosperity. The word *guard* in verse 20 means "to put a hedge around something" or "to set a watch." The word is used over four hundred times in the Old Testament in a number of different ways. In Psalms, it speaks of physical protection, the guarding of life, and the Lord's all-encompassing watchcare of his people. So in the midst of much adversity, God kept David's soul in well-being.

A powerful example of this kind of watchcare is seen in the story of a Christian man by the name of Frederick Nolan. Once during a time of persecution in North Africa, he was fleeing for his life from his enemies; he was pursued by them over hill and valley with no place to hide.

Finally, Nolan fell exhausted into a wayside cave, expecting his enemies to find him soon. As he awaited his death, he saw a spider weaving a web, and within minutes, there was a beautiful web across the mouth of the cave.

The pursuers arrived and wondered if Nolan was hiding in the cave. However, when they saw the unbroken spiderweb, they decided that it was impossible for him to have entered the cave without disturbing the web. So they went on, and Nolan's life was spared. Later, he wrote these words: "Where God is, a spider's web is like a wall. Where God is not, a wall is like a spider's web."[16]

Based on Psalm 34:8–10, the poet composed these lines that speak to the spiritual prosperity that comes through the fear of the Lord:

> O taste and see the Lord is good;
> Those trusting Him are blessed.
> O fear the Lord, saints; none who fear
> Will be with need oppressed.

The lions young may hungry be,
And they may lack their food;
But they who truly seek the Lord
Will not lack any good.[17]

God truly knows how to care for us, protect us, and use us in ways we could never imagine. We see this truth in the life of the early church in Acts 9:31: "So the church throughout all Judea and Galilee and Samaria had peace and was being built up. And walking in the fear of the Lord and in the comfort of the Holy Spirit, it multiplied."

Although walking in the fear of the Lord may not often be considered as a church growth strategy, God certainly honored those early believers as they did so! It seems that this concept was the secret of the early church and the amazing effectiveness God gave it.

Let us never forget his promise for those who fears the Lord: "His soul shall abide in well-being" (Psalm 25:13). To God be the glory for the protection and spiritual prosperity he provides!

Thirdly, the fear of the Lord provides a spiritual legacy. "His offspring shall inherit the land" (Psalm 25:13). The men and women who walk with God will have a vision beyond their own generation and, consequently, be a great blessing to their descendants (see Psalm 102:15–18). However, not everyone has that kind of far-reaching vision; many are only concerned for themselves and fail to see beyond their own lives.

In Isaiah 39, we have the record of a man who failed to maintain the spiritual vision he needed for the coming generations. King Hezekiah had been a very godly and effective king and had experienced God's blessing in extraordinary ways. Yet toward the end of his reign, he made a terrible mistake. Having lost his earlier humility, he showed off his wealth to visiting emissaries from Babylon. It seems he was trusting in his own power and political alliance with a foreign entity rather than trusting in God.

The prophet Isaiah called the king to account for having done so, prophesying that the nation of Judah (and even some of Hezekiah's own sons) would be carried off to Babylon (Isaiah 39:5–7). This was disturbing news indeed! However, the king's response is quite telling:

"Then Hezekiah said to Isaiah, 'The word of the Lord that you have spoken is good.' For he thought, 'There will be peace and security in my days'" (Isaiah 39:8).

Sadly, the king's focus was simply on himself at this point. He seems to show little concern for his own descendants or for his nation. He is just glad that God's judgment would not affect him personally.

Thus, Hezekiah, who had earlier been a role model of faith in God and had experienced his blessing, healing, and deliverance, now ends up as one who shows us how *not* to think and live (see Isaiah 38:1–6). In great contrast to this example, another king was intent on future generations understanding and applying the fear of the Lord. David wrote, "Come, O children, listen to me: I will teach you the fear of the Lord" (Psalm 34:11).

What about us today? Are we interested only in what affects us, or do we have a vision that extends beyond our lifetime to the generations to come? It's true that through our faith and obedience to God, we can affect the lives of those we will never live to see!

We are told that in years past, several multimillionaires left money to themselves in the hope of being brought back to life at a future time. According to a news report, these men arranged to be cryogenically frozen after death. Consequently, they put their wealth in certain trusts, which they believed will be waiting for them when scientists resuscitate them in the future.

Can you imagine thinking that after death, you will eventually be brought back to life so you can retrieve all the assets you stashed away somewhere? It's certainly hard to conceive a believer wanting to do such a thing. Leave heaven and come back to earth? What kind of a deal would that be?

The reality is that no one is coming back for earthly assets left behind at death. However, if we have a vision for the future and are investing our lives in others, our work will continue on even after we are gone. "His offspring shall inherit the land" (Psalm 25:13).

Thank God that through a proper fear of the Lord, we have his promise of spiritual *direction*, spiritual *prosperity*, and a spiritual *legacy*.

So where are we today in our culture in regard to the fear of the Lord? It's seems clear (though it is often denied) that our nation was founded on biblical principles. That's why we see so many Bible verses on government buildings and monuments. However, do you think that Americans by and large have a concept of the fear of the Lord?

Not many years ago, there was a debate in Congress over the so-called Equality Act. One congressman read from the Bible about the difference between men and women. However, another congressman reacted to this by saying, "What any religious tradition describes as God's will is no concern of this Congress."

The second congressman was very wrong for it wasn't a matter of religious tradition being presented. It was biblical truth—something our nation's founders were *very* concerned about. Furthermore, engraved on the wall in that very congressional chamber are the words "In God We Trust."

Hence, members of Congress (and all of us for that matter) would do well to consider the timeless words of Daniel Webster—words that should be sounded and heeded in our culture of moral decadence and utter disregard for the Word of God:

> If we abide by the principles taught in the Bible, our country will go on prospering and to prosper; but if we and our posterity neglect its instructions and authority, no man can tell how sudden a catastrophe may overwhelm us and bury all our glory in profound obscurity.[18]

Certainly, the words of the apostle Paul apply to multitudes in our society today: "There is no fear of God before their eyes" (Romans 3:18).

I have read that the city motto for Glasgow, Scotland, states: "May Glasgow prosper and flourish." At first glance, that seems suitable enough. However, the godly men who originally established the city would not be impressed. The reason is because the complete saying was actually a prayer that said, "May Glasgow prosper and flourish through the preaching of Your Word and the praising of Your Name."

Thus, secular-minded people had removed from the motto the very reason the city *should* prosper and flourish. Moreover, if God and the preaching of his Word are removed from society, the result will be chaos and ultimate judgment and destruction. "It is a fearful thing to fall into the hands of the living God" (Hebrews 10:31).

However, if believers understand and apply the fear of the Lord to their own lives, God will use them to have an extraordinary impact on the watching world around them. You don't have to be a congressman in order to take a bold stand for truth (although we certainly thank God for those who do so). You may be a corporate executive or a blue-collar worker. You may be a senior adult, a college student, or a teenager. Whoever you are, if you've been born again (John 3:6–7), you can stand up for the truth with boldness and love.

For example, one of my seminary professors recounted a memorable story he heard an evangelist tell about Robert Ingersoll, the well-known nineteenth-century agnostic. Ingersoll spoke in cities across the country ridiculing the Christian faith. One night in a Midwestern city, after he had supposedly destroyed any possibility that the Christian faith could be valid, he gave a challenge to his audience.

Ingersoll began by acknowledging his awareness that many Christians come to hear him speak. He then said he would like to know who in the audience that night would still claim to be a Christian even after hearing his presentation. He wondered aloud, "Is there anybody here who will testify, 'I still believe'?"

No one stirred, and Ingersoll laughed out loud. He then gave the challenge a second time, and again no one moved. Once more, Ingersoll laughed. He offered a third challenge, but this time from the back row of the auditorium, two teenage girls stood and began moving out the row and slowly down the aisle, singing, "Stand up, stand up for Jesus, ye soldiers of the cross, lift high his royal banner, it must not suffer loss."

As they walked, others left their rows and followed them until ultimately almost the entire audience was standing as one great throng of people in front of the stage, singing in Ingersoll's face, "Stand up, stand up for Jesus."[19]

We may never find ourselves being publicly challenged by a famous agnostic, but if ever there was a day in our nation when we should reject the fear of man and embrace the fear of God, it is today!

Certainly, we love our country, but as believers, we love God and his eternal kingdom far more. While it is true that America has known incalculable blessing from God in its history, our nation is not invincible. If it continues to reject God's Word and call evil good and good evil (confer Isaiah 5:20), then our beloved nation will incur the judgment of God and, consequently, become just a footnote in world history.

In Joshua 3, God performed a miracle for Israel, and he did it, as Joshua explains to the people, "so that all the peoples of the earth may know that the hand of the Lord is mighty, that you may fear the Lord your God forever" (Joshua 4:24).

Blessed is the nation that understands and accepts this truth. Tragic will be the fall of any nation that ignores it.

CHAPTER 7

Correctly Bearing God's Image

Having considered in the previous chapter the first of two biblical concepts involved in seeking the knowledge of God, we come now to the second concept: the image of God (*the imago Dei*, as it appears in Latin).

Thus, these two scriptural phrases, "the fear of the Lord" and "the image of God," help us better understand what it is meant by the knowledge of God and how he leads his people to correctly seek him and reflect him to others. In other words, these concepts help us understand who God is, who we are, and what his purpose is for us on this earth. For the more we know him, the more we can effectively present him to a culture that, by and large, does not know him at all.

Being made in the image of God is what makes us human and gives us the capacity to relate to our Creator even though that image in us has been shattered due to sin, as we will see shortly. People often excuse their actions, saying, "I'm only human," but there is nothing "only" about being human. We are *truly* human as we reflect the glory of God. John Stonestreet identifies two things at the root of our society's confusion concerning the image of God in human beings:

> First, our culture has forgotten what it means to be human because our culture has forgotten God. Second, the church has neglected to catechize its own about this essential idea. While

most Christians would know *that* every single person is made in the image of God, very few could articulate or explain *what it means* to bear God's image, how the world is different because of the imago dei within it, and the implications of the imago dei for the various layers of society.[1]

Let me suggest three keys to understanding this remarkable phrase "the image of God." They are: the summit of creation, the reality of disruption, and the grace of restoration.

The Summit of *Creation*

In the creation account, we read these words: "Then God said, 'Let us make man in our image, after our likeness'" (Genesis 1:26). Previously, in his creative acts, God had simply said, "Let there be..." As a result, light, darkness, land, sea, skies, plants, and animals all came about instantly. However, on the sixth day of creation, God said, "Let us make man." Thus, the creation story became delightfully *personal*. As we see in Genesis 2:7, God breathed into man "the breath of life, and the man became a living creature" (or "being" in NASB, CSB).

Furthermore, Genesis 1:27 states, "So God created man in his own image, in the image of God he created him; male and female he created them." Thus, here is what we can call the *summit* of God's creation—humanity created in his own image.

The Hebrew words for *image* and *likeness* mean that God would make a creature similar but not identical to himself. Thus, when God said, "Let us make man in our image, after our likeness" (Genesis 1:26), it "simply would have meant to the original readers, as Wayne Grudem points out, "Let us make man to be *like* us and to *represent* us."[2]

Consequently, to be made in God's image points, first of all, to who he is in his essence. Our likeness to God is not physical, of course, for he is spirit (Exodus 33:20; 1 Timothy 6:16; 1 John 4:12) while at the same time being triune in his person as Father, Son, and

Holy Spirit. Thus, the God of plurality has created humans with plurality in that we are body, soul, and spirit. In fact, in Genesis 1:26, we have the first clear indication in the Bible of the triunity of God or what we would call the Trinity ("Let *us* make man in *our* image, after *our* likeness," emphasis mine).

To be made in God's image also means that because we have a soul, we are eternal as God himself is eternal. However, unlike us who are the created ones with a beginning, God is the *uncreated* one who is without beginning. Furthermore, because God is personal in nature (with a mind, heart, and will), we are like him in this regard and, as a result, can be in relationship with him. In fact, this is why we have a spirit—that we might have fellowship with the eternal God who is spirit. As the Westminster Shorter Catechism (1647) states, "Man's chief end is to glorify God and to enjoy him forever."

What a blessing and privilege to live out this extraordinary truth each day! Truly, the most important thing we do in our lives is to seek the Lord, loving, praising, thanking, and obeying him. Therefore, this daily fellowship with God is the most essential facet of our existence on this earth and forms the very basis for our thoughts, words, attitudes, and actions.

Furthermore, the fact that humans are made in the image of God is not true of any other creature in all of God's creation. Therefore, this is what makes humanity unique among all of God's creatures, and subsequently, humans can relate to him in a way that the other created beings cannot. Warren Wiersbe explains the implications of this reality:

> It is inconsistent for people who do not believe we were created by God in His image to want to exalt man. If man is just an animal, then why not let him live like an animal? Why have standards? Why have Laws? Why does society need protection if we are only animals? It is inconsistent. The fact that we are made in God's image means we have dignity. We are not just animals.[3]

It is also important to see that God ordained for man to rule over the creation ("have dominion," Genesis 1:26). Interestingly, toward the end of the Bible, we see that God's redeemed people will reign (Revelation 22:5). Thus, having made every person in his own image, God has revealed his intent for humans to rule and, ultimately, for redeemed persons to reign.

Thus, in being given dominion over God's creation, Adam and Eve were to represent him as his image-bearers. Because his instruction was for them to be fruitful and multiply (Genesis 1:28), it is obvious that God intended the earth to be filled with men and women who would pursue the knowledge of God and worship and serve him in love and obedience. Even after the fall, this command to fill the earth was to be carried out through Noah and his descendants (Genesis 9:1, 7).

Moreover, it is clear in the first two chapters of Genesis that because Adam and Eve were the first parents, there is only one race, as Paul says in Acts 17:26, "He made from one man every nation of mankind to live on all the face of the earth." This certainly gives us the clear basis for rejecting any form of racism for all ethnic groups throughout the world have come from one man.

As we ponder God's remarkable plan and purpose for humanity, let us stand in awe with King David who prayed, "What is man that you are mindful of him, and the son of man that you care for him? Yet you have made him a little lower than the heavenly beings and crowned him with glory and honor" (Psalm 8:4–5). Could there be a greater pronouncement of human dignity?

We should also note that man and woman are made *in* God's image, not *as* God's image; that is to say, there is something in them that reflects the being and character of God. So when Scripture speaks of man being made in the image of God, it is not talking about the human body for there is nothing physical or visible about humans that can be part of the image of the invisible, spiritual God.

Consequently, it was wrong for the great artist Michelangelo to depict God the Creator on the ceiling of the Sistine Chapel as a man with long white hair and a beard. In my view, the artist was, in fact, violating the second of the Ten Commandments in doing so. God is simply not to be communicated in that way.

Yet while God the Father does not have physical, visible form (John 6:46), it is true that he has revealed himself in his Son. John 1:18 says, "No one has ever seen God; the only God, who is at the Father's side, he has made him known." Thus, in seeing Jesus, the people were seeing God himself in the flesh (see also John 14:6–11).

Thus, the image of God is not about human form or a human body; it's about something else. It has to do with what the apostle Peter calls "the hidden person of the heart" (1 Peter 3:4). It is in this hidden person that the image of God is to be found. This is why David prays, "Behold, you delight in truth in the inward being, and you teach me wisdom in the secret heart" (Psalm 51:6).

Consequently, in contrast to the world's emphasis, the value of human beings is not in the physical appearance of the body. Rather, the value of a person is in that which forms the soul or inward being (see 2 Corinthians 4:16) for it is here that the image of God is reflected.

In the New Testament, we see three elements that are named in this image: righteousness, holiness, and knowledge (Ephesians 4:24; Colossians 3:10). Therefore, a man is capable of displaying these characteristics because of being created in God's image. However, it all starts with knowing God. This is why he created humans in his image in the first place: that they might know him and be known *by* him. As J. I. Packer put it: "What matters supremely is not the fact that I know God, but the fact that he knows me."

Furthermore, it is only as we grow in the knowledge of the Lord that we can truly enjoy him and reflect his glory to those around us British pastor F. B. Meyer prayed: "Keep me from fashioning you for myself, God my Savior, after my own imaginings. May I not make a graven image of you, but know you as you are."[4]

The first key then to understanding the image of God has to do with the summit of creation, thus revealing the inestimable value of man and woman because of God's creation of them in his image. Let's consider the second key.

The Reality of *Disruption*

This disruption, of course, occurred in the garden of Eden when man sinned against God; when that happened, his spirit died, and he became separated from his Creator. What happened to the image of God in man at that point? It wasn't eradicated (Genesis 9:6; James 3:9), but it was marred. It was shattered. As a result, this damaged image would be passed on to the entire human race that was yet to come. The apostle Paul makes clear the horrendous results of sin as he refers to unredeemed people:

> They are darkened in their understanding, excluded from the life of God, because of the ignorance that is in them and because of the hardness of their hearts. They became callous and gave themselves over to promiscuity for the practice of every kind of impurity with a desire for more and more. (Ephesians 4:18–19 CSB)

Similarly, many other passages show the deadly results of sin (e.g., Proverbs 21:4, 26:24–26; Luke 12:15; Galatians 5:19; Ephesians 2:1–3; 1 John 2:9–11). Thus, Adam and Eve did not lose God's image, but they lost their innocence, and life on this planet has never been the same again. This reality led C. S. Lewis to comment that nearly all we call human history is "the long terrible story of man trying to find something other than God which will make him happy."[5]

For example, the Enlightenment of the nineteenth century brought a sweeping spirit of optimism, spawning the humanistic idea that man no longer needs God in order to understand his origin, identity, and purpose. Instead, there arose the belief that humans were on the verge of a utopia brought about through education, science, and economics, thus proving (in the minds of many) that the pinnacle of evolution had at long last arrived. Thus, many people saw this development leading to the eradication of crime, war, and poverty. Furthermore, an end to disease was anticipated as the result of advancing medical developments.

However, World War I certainly revealed the fallacy of such foolish humanism—at least until a positive spin emerged: *the war to end all wars*. However, as R. C. Sproul has pointed out: "Somebody forgot to tell that to the sons of Lamech: Mussolini, Tojo, Stalin, Mao, and the corporal from Bavaria. The 20th century brought a new horror to world history, the phenomenon of global war."[6]

The failure to find true peace and fulfillment is due to our rebellion against God and his commands. Through Satan's deception, we have pursued our own glory and enjoyment apart from acknowledging our Creator and seeking his glory alone. Is this not evident in our culture today? It seems that it has changed to the point where that which was considered unthinkable not very long ago has now become incontestable!

Thus, in recent times, our nation has been referred to as post-Christian. However, it seems that in many ways, a post-*Christian* America has now become a post-*sanity* America. For that which is called progress today is often the exact opposite of the kind of success and spiritual advancement defined and described in the Bible. Consider the timely words of G. K. Chesterton (1874–1936), which sound quite prophetic in light of the way the term *progressive* is used in our day.

> What a man knows now is that the whole march of mankind can turn and tramp backwards in its tracks; that progress can start progressing, or feeling as if it were progressing, in precisely the contrary course from that which has been called progress for centuries.[7]

Similarly, Horatius Bonar described the devil's strategy by saying, "Progress, progress, progress, is his watchword now, by means of which he hopes to allure men away from the old anchorages, under the pretext of giving them wider, fuller, more genial teachings."[8] Amazingly, those "up-to-date" words were written 150 years ago!

Clearly, the image of God becoming distorted within us has brought devastating results throughout history. Evangelist Vance

Havner gave a striking illustration of this reality when he described the time he sat in a city motel and watched on television astronauts taking off for the moon:

> I could turn around in my chair and look out my window at a park across the street where I dared not walk for fear of thugs and thieves. In vivid contrast I beheld the wonder of man's ingenuity on one hand and the moral depravity of man on the other. While three men race toward the stars, other men creep in the slime. Astronauts and anarchists! While some travel to the moon I cannot walk in the park![9]

Now there is good news, which we will come to presently, but as you might imagine, a failure to understand what it means to be created in God's image has resulted in a terrible devaluing of human life. For we live in a day when the populace, by and large, is either tragically ignorant of the truth of being made in the image of God or ignores it altogether.

The abortion holocaust is certainly an example of the muddled and evil thinking of our day—a thinking that flows from an evolutionary and humanistic worldview. In a day when we are lectured about listening to the "science," it seems that many of those same voices say little or nothing about the science that shows a baby's heart beginning to beat at eighteen days and pumping blood within twenty-two days.

It is also true that babies in the womb respond to touch, have observable brain waves at six weeks, and develop distinctive fingerprints at about nine or ten weeks. As Randy Alcorn points out, "In the Bible there are references to born children and unborn children, but there is no such thing as potential, incipient, or 'almost' children."[10] Moreover, Gordon J. Keddie sums up the deadly thinking of our radical culture today:

> It speaks volumes of the state of our world that so many regard children as an unwanted

inconvenience and that so many governments support this with legislation that permits and promotes the killing of children before they are born! The so-called "right to choose" is no better than a "license to kill." It effectively places the life of an unborn child no higher than a diseased appendix or an ingrown toenail![11]

Another example of cultural insanity is reflected in the comments of Ingrid Newkirk, the controversial cofounder of People for the Ethical Treatment of Animals (PETA). Newkirk has stated, "There is no rational reason for saying that a human being has special rights. A rat is a pig is a dog is a boy."[12]

Newkirk told the *Washington Post* that the atrocities of Nazi Germany pale by comparison to killing animals for food. She made this mind-boggling comparison: "Six million Jews died in concentration camps, but six billion broiler chickens will die this year in slaughterhouses."[13] Evidently, Newkirk is not alone in her views. In fact, author Richard E. Simmons III has reported: "There are a number of ethicists who argue now that an animal's rights should take precedence over a human's."[14]

As shocking as these assertions are, they are the logical outflow of evolutionary philosophy. If we simply evolved with no intelligent design necessary then, as John MacArthur writes, "We ourselves are ultimately no better than or different from any other living species. We are nothing more than protoplasm waiting to become manure."[15] MacArthur goes on to say:

> A worldview that outright denies a Creator who made male and female in his own image is a deadly one for it will ultimately lead to a total disregard for the value of human life. And there are those who have even suggested the benefits of voluntary human extinction, believing that this will solve all of earth's problems by allowing the survival of the other species of life![16]

This extremely disturbing view of humankind that MacArthur exposes can actually be traced back to Charles Darwin. As Simmons points out, the key idea in Darwin's book is how good it is for the least favored races to become extinct. This kind of blatant racism is plainly seen in the complete title of the book: *The Origin of Species by Means of Natural Selection or the Preservation of Favoured Races in the Struggle for Life.*[17]

Obviously, humanistic evolutionary theory has continued to the present day, permeating our institutions of higher learning. Consequently, if radical secularists have their way, the value of human life will continue to diminish and the rights of animals will supersede those of people.

Yet the Bible is clear that every person has been made in the image of God. Animals, no. Persons, yes! To reject this truth is to reject the God who created us and the Christ who came to save us and to prefer instead that of living in our fallenness rather than seeking the forgiveness and life found only in Christ.

Thus, as C. S. Lewis put it, "Fallen man is not simply an imperfect creature who needs improvement: he is a rebel who must lay down his arms."[18]

To understand then what it means to be made in the image of God is not only to recognize our responsibility to God himself but to also recognize our responsibility to other people. Consequently, from preborn children to the elderly, every person is equally worthy of dignity, honor, and protection. John Stott summarizes superbly the false thinking in our culture and the solution for it:

> Those who regard a human being as nothing but a programmed machine (behaviorists) or an absurdity (existentialists) or a naked ape (humanistic evolutionists) are all denigrating our creation in God's image. True, we are also rebels against God and deserve nothing at his hand except judgment, but our fallenness has not entirely destroyed our God-likeness. More important still, in spite of our revolt against him,

God has loved, redeemed, adopted, and recreated us in Christ.[19]

Hence, we are not without hope—*glorious* hope—as we will now explore.

The Grace of *Restoration*

The last key to understanding the image of God is good news—in fact, the best news ever! The marred image of God—due to the fall of man in the garden of Eden—has been restored through Jesus Christ for all who believe in him (John 5:24).

By God's grace, people can be forgiven, cleansed, and restored through the atoning death and bodily resurrection of Jesus from the dead. Yes, all of us were born in Adam, but by God's grace, we who know Jesus have been born again in him. We were dead in our sins but have now been raised to new life in Christ. Consider the moving words written by John Henry Newman in 1886:

> O loving wisdom of our God!
> When all was sin and shame,
> a second Adam to the fight
> and to the rescue came.
>
> O wisest love! That flesh and blood,
> which did in Adam fail,
> should strive afresh against the foe,
> should strive, and should prevail.

Yes, Adam failed, but Jesus prevailed! Because he did, we not only have forgiveness of sin but an eternity with him. Referring to the Incarnation, Glen Scrivener writes, "Jesus comes to stand at the intersection of heaven and earth. He sums up all humanity in order to put right what Adam got wrong."[20]

We know this is completely true because the apostle Paul declares in 1 Corinthians 15:21–22, "For as by a man came death, by a man has come also the resurrection of the dead. For as in Adam all die, so also in Christ shall all be made alive." So you could put it like this: Adam went to *his* tree (with its forbidden fruit) in selfishness and pride, and the result was utter disaster for humanity. Jesus went to *his* tree (the cross) and, in doing so, reversed the curse.

Subsequently, true spiritual restoration comes only through Jesus Christ who alone paid sin's penalty on the cross. For no other means of acceptance with God and the assurance of eternal redemption is offered. Moreover, because we have a victorious Savior and a transforming message, we can proclaim with the hymn writer:

> Come, ye sinners, poor and needy,
> weak and wounded, sick and sore;
> Jesus ready stands to save you,
> full of pity, love, and pow'r.
>
> Come, ye weary, heavy laden,
> lost and ruined by the fall;
> if you tarry till you're better,
> you will never come at all.[21]

Thus, Dr. Martyn Lloyd-Jones wrote: "Man's first and greatest need is not to be improved; it is not to be given better advantages; it is not to be healed physically. Man's primary need is to be reconciled to God."[22]

The good news of the gospel is that this reconciliation is available through the Lord Jesus Christ (and *only* through him); he will never turn away those who come to him in true repentance and faith. He says, "All that the Father gives me will come to me, and whoever comes to me I will never cast out" (John 6:37).

Neither will Christ ever abandon those who know him—a promise that brings great contentment regardless of circumstances. He says, "I will never leave you nor forsake you" (Hebrews 13:5). In fact, since several negatives in the Greek are employed here, the words of Jesus can be paraphrased: "There is absolutely no way whatsoever that I will ever, ever leave you."[23]

Thus, we give thanks to God that through the atoning death of Christ, the curse of sin is reversed for all who trust in him. As Romans 8:1 declares, "There is therefore now no condemnation for those who are in Christ Jesus." The Greek word in this verse for *no* is very strong, thereby emphasizing that there is absolutely no condemnation hanging over us whatsoever!

Think of it! No sin—past, present, or future—can ever be charged against us as believers for sin's penalty was paid by Christ. Furthermore, his righteousness has been imputed to us.

> For our sake he made him to be sin who
> knew no sin, so that in him we might become the
> righteousness of God. (2 Corinthians 5:21)

This is indeed an amazing statement! Jesus became sin so we could become righteous. In other words, our sins are charged to *his* account in order that his righteousness can be credited to *our* account. This is why Jesus took our place on the cross, sacrificing his life for us. Pastor Louie Giglio has written:

> Every wrong you have done and every wrong
> that has been done to you has been swallowed up
> in every right that Jesus has done and in every
> wrong that has been done to him.[24]

The penalty of sin has been fully paid; therefore, as believers, we are now declared *not guilty*! Furthermore, God will never change that word of acquittal. Thus, you could say that it was through the finished work of Jesus on the cross and his resurrection from the dead that God ceased pressing charges against us! We now have a perfect standing before him in the righteousness of Christ himself. As Herman Ridderbos put it, "In the death of Christ, we see God's condemnation of sin, but in the resurrection, we see God's acquittal of sinners."[25]

Indeed, that's restoration! As a result, there's not a scintilla of guilt hanging over us. As believers, we can truthfully say that our permanent address is *in Christ* (Ephesians 1:4–5) and our joy throughout eternity, as now, will be that of *no condemnation* and *no separation* (Romans 8:1, 38–39). Ponder Charles Wesley's moving words:

> No condemnation now I dread:
> Jesus, and all in Him is mine!
> Alive in Him, my living Head,
> And clothed in righteousness divine;
> Bold I approach the eternal throne
> And claim the crown,
> through Christ, my own.[26]

Furthermore, a day is coming when God's children will live in a world where everything has been restored, where the wolf will dwell with the lamb (Isaiah 11:6), and men's weapons will be turned into plowshares (Isaiah 2:4). Thank God for the coming city "that has foundations, whose designer and builder is God" (Hebrews 11:10). Augustine, bishop of Hippo, said, "That which man builds man destroys, but the city of God is built by God and cannot be destroyed by man."[27]

Yes, in that glorious, coming day, we will have new bodies without pain, suffering, and tears. In perfect bodies living in a perfect place, we will never again experience temptation, suffering, grief, separations from loved ones and friends, and tragedies of any kind. Even death itself will have been destroyed (1 Corinthians 15:26)!

> Crown Him the Lord of life,
> who triumphed o'er the grave,
> And rose victorious in the strife
> for those He came to save.
> His glories now we sing,
> who died, and rose on high,
> Who died eternal life to bring,
> and lives that death may die.[28]

Indeed! Jesus *lives that death may die.* Therefore, in the new world that is coming, there will be no mortuaries or cemeteries. Neither hospitals nor pharmacies. Doctors and undertakers? Out of a job! Preachers as well.

However, this will be exactly as it should be. In that day, our present responsibilities will be over, and we will have new ones that will be perfectly meaningful and fulfilling throughout all eternity. So in that sense, no one will be out of a job in heaven!

Furthermore, Jesus "will transform our lowly body to be like his glorious body, by the power that enables him even to subject all things to himself" (Philippians 3:21). Yes, one day, Jesus will change our bodies so that they are like his resurrection body. Because he has all authority and all power, he can do this...and he *will* do it. As theologian D. A. Carson has said, "We aren't suffering from anything that a good resurrection can't fix." Thanks be to God that such a resurrection is in our future!

> Beloved, we are God's children now, and
> what we will be has not yet appeared; but we
> know that when he appears we shall be like him,
> because we shall see him as he is. (1 John 3:2)

The great preacher G. Campbell Morgan said, "I never begin my work in the morning without thinking that perhaps He may interrupt my work and begin His own. I am not looking for death—I am looking for Him."[29]

Physical death is not the end! Recall the words of Jesus to Martha, "I am the resurrection and the life. Whoever believes in me, though he die, yet shall he live, and everyone who lives and believes in me shall never die" (John 11:25–26). Because of who Jesus is and what he has done, believers will live with him throughout eternity.

The fact that we will live again is no more incredible than the fact that we live at all. Since God brought us into this world, he is able to take us into the next one! He who had the power to make us *once* has the power to make us *again.* Therefore, we live because Jesus lives, we overcome because he overcame, we will rise because he rose, and we will reign because he reigns!

The world, however, looks at a dead body and says, "That's the end. It's over for him." In fact, the Roman Marcus Aurelius believed that at death, all that is left is dust, ashes, bones, and stench. Do you think he was a very happy guy? I'm glad we have more to look forward to than that! Os Guinness has perceptively written:

> Time and history have meaning. Under the twin truths of God's sovereignty and human significance, time and history are going somewhere, and each of us is not only unique and significant in ourselves, but we have a unique and significant part to play in our own lives, in our own generation, and therefore in the overall sweep of history... We are not dust blowing in the wind. We are not a freak accident lost in a universe that came to be without meaning and one day will cease to be without meaning.[30]

Thank God for the unshakable hope that is ours as children of the living God!

Several years ago, I was making a purchase in a clothing store. The clerk asked for a driver's license ID and said that she needed my birthday and my expiration date. I told her that I could give her my birthday but that I did not know when I would expire! What she really meant, of course, was that she needed the expiration date of my license. However, I don't think I'll ever forget the way her statement came out!

The truth is that all of us will *expire* unless Jesus returns in our lifetime. Yet, we need not be afraid for he has conquered death, and because he has done so, physical death is gain for the believer! "For me, to live is Christ and to die is gain" (Philippians 1:21 CSB).

> It is not death to die, to leave this weary road,
> and join the saints who dwell on high,

who've found their home with God.
It is not death to close the eyes
long dimmed by tears, and wake in joy
before Your throne, delivered from our fears.[31]

Therefore, we as believers are not in the land of the living on our way to the land of the dying, as many people would conclude. Rather, we are in the land of the dying on our way to the land of the living!

When Marco Polo, the famous traveler of the thirteenth century, was dying, people urged him to recant—that is, to withdraw the amazing stories he had told about China and the Far East. However, far from recanting, he declared, "I have not told half what I saw."

Likewise, who could even begin to imagine or describe the future God has prepared for those who know him? Yet one thing is for sure: he has it all planned out, and it is a glorious future indeed.

There is a land of pure delight,
where saints immortal reign;
infinite day excludes the night,
and pleasures banish pain.[32]

Yes, the great day of full restoration is coming for every true child of God. Theologian J. I. Packer put it quite memorably:

Hearts on earth say in the course of a joyful experience, "I don't want this ever to end." But it invariably does. The hearts of those in heaven say, "I want this to go on forever." And it will. There can be no better news than this.[33]

It is an irrepressible joy to know that as believers, we have been forgiven the *penalty* of sin and have been granted *power* over sin. Furthermore, in the day that is coming, we won't even know the *presence* of sin! It will be a day of perfect freedom, glorious worship, unspeakable joy, and unending fellowship with our risen, ascended, and reigning Lord. Little wonder then that William Jenkyn declared, "To forsake Christ for the world is to leave a treasure for a trifle, eternity for a moment, reality for a shadow."[34]

As God's image-bearers, we rejoice in the restoration he has given us through Christ. We also rejoice in the work of renewal God continues to do in our lives on a daily basis. The apostle Paul declares that as we behold the glory of the Lord, we "are being transformed into the same image from one degree of glory to another" (2 Corinthians 3:18). That's quite a thought, isn't it? We have the opportunity to grow in the image of God every day—an image that has been restored in us through the work of the Holy Spirit.

Furthermore, we rejoice in the privilege of proclaiming to others the saving and restoring work of Jesus Christ through his death and resurrection. Be challenged and encouraged by the following words:

> The Lord means to save a vast number of people before this world is done. To this end, the *separateness* of God's people—their love for Jesus Christ, their personal godliness, including their repentance for sin and faith in Christ as their Savior, their humility and service, their prayer and love for people—has a powerful impact on the world.[35]

May God give us courage to go through every door he opens and boldness to proclaim the gospel regardless of opposition. As Vance Havner said, "It is not our business to make the message acceptable but to make it available. We are not to see that they like it, but that they get it."

Let us then seek to remain a usable instrument in the hand of the Lord so that he may spread the truth of his living Word to those ensnared by cultural insanity and in the darkness of spiritual oppression.

> O that I had a thousand voices
> To praise my God with a thousand tongues!

My heart, which in the Lord rejoices,
Would then proclaim in grateful songs
To all, wherever I might be,
What great things God has done for me![36]

Let us regularly review the two crucially important concepts of these last two chapters: the fear of the Lord and the image of God. As stated in chapter 6, these are two key doctrines that help us better understand who God is, who we are, and what his purpose is for us on this earth.

God gives us the wonderful privilege to grow in our understanding of these concepts and the power to effectively communicate them to others in a day when our culture, by and large, is woefully ignorant of such liberating truth.

CONCLUSION

Thinking Rightly...Living Boldly...Trusting Fully...

John Adams once wrote to Thomas Jefferson, saying, "My friend, you and I have lived in serious times."[1] Indeed, they had. Moreover, who could doubt that we today live in serious times? In fact, *perilous* times—a day in which our culture has lost its mind. The Old Testament prophet Isaiah pronounced woe on those "who call evil good and good evil" (Isaiah 5:20). Tragically, the utter moral confusion of *that* day is being lived out in *our* day.

Furthermore, the Christian worldview is constantly being opposed and demeaned, especially in institutions of higher education. Scholar Roy Aldrich once described what has been a sad reality for many years now:

> Satan does not waste his ammunition. Professors, who are being paid to teach philosophy, English, biology, mathematics...often take time from their class periods to undermine the Bible and orthodox Christianity. Why are they not doing the same with the sacred books of other religions? The answer is that Satan, the original liar, is sympathetic with books that lie. His real enmity is directed against the book of

161

truth because it contains the dynamite for his defeat.[2]

The reality, however, is that it's not just university classrooms where Satan's deceptions are evident. He will use every means possible to twist and malign the truth, whether in a school, on television and the Internet, in the halls of Congress, or even in a church setting where full commitment to the authority of the Bible is not clearly taught and practiced.

Therefore, believers must be on the alert at all times for the devil "prowls around like a roaring lion, seeking someone to devour" (1 Peter 5:8). The apostle Peter goes on to tell us, "Resist him, firm in the faith, knowing that the same kind of sufferings are being experienced by your fellow believers throughout the world" (1 Peter 5:9 CSB).

As former British Prime Minister Margaret Thatcher once famously said to President George H. W. Bush during the Gulf War: "This is no time to go wobbly." Such a reminder is greatly needed in our own day for all who would boldly move forward in faith—regardless of massive cultural changes in ideology and governmental policies. May the following words (written anonymously) never be said of us:

> There was a very cautious man
> who never laughed or played.
> He never risked, he never tried,
> he never sang or prayed.
> And when one day he passed away
> his insurance was denied,
> for since he never really lived,
> they claimed he never died.

Let us live in such a way that no one will be able to rightfully question where our allegiances lay!

It has been said that "culture is perhaps best defined as the world in which we live and the world that lives in us."[3] The problem, of course, is when the culture living in Christians reflects the world more than the teaching of Scripture. Sadly, many in the church have so given into secular thinking that, as historian Mark Noll observed, the scandal of the evangelical mind is that there is not much of an evangelical mind.[4]

Apparently, Charles Spurgeon observed the prevalence of this problem in his day. He told about a man who was asked how things went at a particular church meeting. He replied, "Oh, it was lovely. None of us knew anything, and we all taught each other."[5] Regrettably, many professing Christians and churches in our day have also departed from the careful study of the essentials of the Christian faith, and tragically, they are leading others to do the same.

The experience of Lesslie Newbigin provides a telling commentary on the reality to which Noll and Spurgeon point. As a missionary from England, Newbigin spent forty years serving in India during the twentieth century. By God's grace, he had an effective ministry as he faithfully spent those years contextually proclaiming the gospel in all of its beauty and power. However, when Newbigin returned home, he experienced a culture shock greater than anything he had encountered in India. It was the shock of not only witnessing the changes that had taken place in his own country but, even more ominously, the dramatic impact the culture had on the churches.

Thus, it was clear to him that a culture of secularism and humanism had influenced the thinking of professing Christians, thus rendering the church weak and, consequently, powerless to confront the destructive issues of society at that time. To a great degree, is this not the case in our own day? Perhaps we should ask, which do our lives and churches reflect the most? The culture around us or the Christ within us?

As a result of the disturbing development Lesslie Newbigin found when he returned to his home country of England, he spent the rest of his life boldly speaking the truth of Scripture, just as he had faithfully done in India. We must do the same, lovingly and courageously proclaiming the truth of God's Word in the power of the Holy Spirit.

Pastor and humorist Charles Lowery tells about a friend of his who was house-training his dog. Every time the dog made a mess in the house, the man would hit the dog with a paper and throw the dog out the window. After about three weeks, Lowery asked his friend how it was going. The man said, "The dumb dog…he makes a mess and then jumps out the window."

Just like that dog, it's easy for us to learn the wrong thing over time, especially in today's confused and chaotic culture with its pervasive influence. As theologian Carl F. H. Henry said, "Not to be fortified with good ideas is to be victimized by bad ones."

Consequently, learning to think biblically is of the utmost importance for this is the kind of thinking that reflects a scriptural worldview about the nature of God, the fallenness of human beings, the person and work of Christ, salvation by grace alone, and God's mighty work throughout history.

Therefore, because we have the power of the written Word (1 Thessalonians 2:13) and the presence of the living Christ (Matthew 28:20), we need not shrink in fear even in the midst of a culture spiraling downward. As followers of Jesus, we must be vigilant to remember our calling to live as sojourners and exiles (1 Peter 2:11). We must steadfastly keep our gaze on our eternal King who, out of immeasurable love, died to pay the penalty for our sin. Major Ian Thomas succinctly put it like this: "All there is of God is available to the man who is available to all there is of God."

The great New England theologian Jonathan Edwards certainly wanted to be that kind of man, and he pointed to the day in which he made a full dedication of himself to God. Edwards wrote:

> On January 12, 1723, I made a solemn dedication of myself to God, and wrote it down; giving up myself, and all that I had to God; to be for the future, in no respect, my own; to act as one that had no right to be himself, in any respect. And solemnly vowed to take God for my whole portion and felicity; looking on nothing else, as any part of my happiness.[6]

164

Therefore, ask God to help you live as a true pilgrim on this earth so that although you are *in* the world, the evidence will be clear that you are not *of* the world. Heed daily the words of 1 Thessalonians 5:21–22, "Test everything; hold fast what is good. Abstain from every form of evil." Author and former missions executive David Platt has written words similar to those which Jonathan Edwards penned in his dedication to God three centuries earlier.

> We can assent to the spirit of this age and choose to spend our lives seeking worldly pleasures, acquiring worldly possessions, and pursuing worldly ambitions—all under the banner of cultural Christianity. Or we can decide that Jesus is worth more than this. We can recognize that he has created us, saved us, and called us for a much greater purpose than anything this world could ever offer us. We can die to ourselves, our hopes, our dreams, our ambitions, our priorities, and our plans. We can do all of this because we believe that the person and the plan of Christ bring reward that makes any risk more than worth it.[7]

Hymn writer William Williams expressed the godly vision and commitment of both Edwards and Platt (and countless others throughout the centuries) in beautiful poetic form:

> Jesus, Jesus, all sufficient,
> Beyond telling is Thy worth;
> In Thy Name lie greater treasures
> Than the richest found on earth.[8]

Certainly, there are those who will not understand or appreciate the beliefs we cherish and the biblical principles upon which we stand. However, our commitment to God and his Word is more than worth any risk involved.

The great German reformer Martin Luther was one who surely knew about risk as he proclaimed the truth of Scripture in a dark and dangerous time. In the small university town of Wittenberg, Germany, he had boldly posted his *95 Theses* on the church door, exposing the deadly corruption of the medieval church. It was a remarkable turning point in history. It also made him a marked and hunted man.

Nevertheless, Luther was committed to the Word of God regardless of any endangerment his convictions might bring for he knew the power of the Bible to change lives. As a result, true reformation ultimately spread across the continent! In his famous hymn, "A Mighty Fortress Is Our God" (inspired by Psalm 46), Luther spoke of God's truth as "that word above all earthly powers." He went on to declare:

> Let goods and kindred go,
> This mortal life also;
> The body they may kill:
> God's truth abideth still:
> His kingdom is forever.[9]

Yes, indeed! That word *above all earthly powers* is stronger than all the forces Satan can marshal. As Aleksandr Solzhenitsyn declared, "One word of truth shall outweigh the whole world."[10] God's Word is timeless and timely and, therefore, to this day *abideth still*, as Luther put it. "The grass withers, the flower fades, but the word of our God will stand forever" (Isaiah 40:8).

> Rejoice, believer, in the Lord,
> who makes your cause His own;
> the hope that's built upon his Word
> shall ne'er be overthrown.[11]

In a book of letters to young pastors, Calvin Miller states: "Define your times. Treasure your calling. Pray without ceasing.

The terrors of the age are less than the grandeur of the Christ within you."[12]

What a helpful insight for young and old, pastors and laypeople alike—an insight we should keep constantly in our minds and on our hearts. Therefore, let us seek to understand the times in which we live. Above all, let us seek to understand more and more the God whom we worship, and let us serve and follow the Christ whose grandeur within us is beyond all human comprehension. It will do wonders in freeing us from the terrors of the age!

Having seen the supreme importance of pursuing the knowledge of God, read once again the words of Hosea 6:3, "Let us know; let us press on to know the Lord." For to learn more about knowing God and continually growing in that knowledge is truly our highest privilege in life.

At the same time, we must realize that it is possible to grow in knowledge while not growing in grace. For example, we have all met people who have a great deal of Bible knowledge, but no one can get along with them! People who grow in knowledge but fail to apply that knowledge to their lives so that it becomes wisdom will not grow in grace. It's just knowledge in their heads that they use to try to impress others, thus revealing the dangerous disconnect between head and heart with the consequent result of sinful pride. However, when we are growing in knowledge *and* grace, we will experience true spiritual growth. This pleases God and brings forth fruit from our lives.

Moreover, God's ultimate plan is for every believer to be conformed to the image of Christ (Romans 8:29). We have become a new creation in him (2 Corinthians 5:17), and we "have put off the old self with its practices and have put on the new self, which is being renewed in knowledge after the image of its creator" (Colossians 3:10).

Now while we certainly rejoice in this amazing renewal, we remain fully aware of our susceptibility to temptation and sin due to living in earthly bodies. So every day we should seek to follow Christ more closely, pray more fervently, read and meditate on his living

Word more deeply, and avail ourselves of the whole armor of God (see appendix 1).

Furthermore, the deteriorating condition of today's culture demands all the more that we who are in Christ stand unified, draw encouragement from our fellow believers, and hold one another accountable in our walk with God.

A page from church history illustrates the vital importance of unity in the life of the church. The great eighteenth-century evangelist George Whitefield once stepped into a stagecoach about to leave Edinburgh. A lady who belonged to a different denomination happened to step into the same coach. Upon seeing Whitefield, she became alarmed, saying, "Are you not Mr. Whitefield?"

"Yes, madam," he replied.

She then exclaimed, "Oh, then let me get out."

Whitefield calmly replied, "Surely, madam. But before you go, let me ask you one question. Suppose you die and go to heaven, and then suppose I die and go there also, when I come in, will you go out?"

The lady was struck by his words. She then cordially shook his hand, and they proceeded together on their journey.[13]

Thus, unity in Christ is not based on denominationalism but rather on Christ himself. As believers, we are one in him through his atoning death on the cross and his bodily resurrection from the dead. And to be one in him is to be one with all others throughout the world who are one in him! Moreover, in John 17, Jesus prayed for this supremely important oneness among his followers:

> Holy Father, keep them in your name, which you have given me, that they may be *one*, even as we are *one*... I do not ask that you take them out of the world, but that you keep them from the evil one. (John 17:11, 15, emphasis mine)

Therefore, let us pursue the knowledge of God through all the means of grace available to us so that, as Paul says, we will be "transformed into the same image from one degree of glory to another" (2 Corinthians 3:18).

Only a high view of God and the constant transformation he brings can keep us from an attitude of defeatism in a culture such as ours. If our view of him is not accurate, then people can appear intimidating and the influence of culture overwhelming. Thus, Scripture compels us to see God as he is in his glory, majesty, and power. Yes, the times are perilous, but as Dietrich Bonhoeffer said so well, "May God in his mercy lead us through these times; but above all, may he lead us to himself."

Furthermore, let us ask God for opportunities to lovingly proclaim the truth of Scripture to others so they will come to faith in Christ and escape the snare of the devil in the midst of a culture gone awry. Though the image of God is distorted, it is still there in every person. That doesn't mean that every person is saved; it *does* mean, however, that every person was created in the likeness and image of God (as we saw in the previous chapter). This is why C. S. Lewis wrote in *The Weight of Glory*:

> There are no ordinary people. You have never talked to a mere mortal.
>
> Nations, cultures, arts, civilization—these are mortal, and their life is to ours as the life of a gnat. But it is immortals whom we joke with, work with, marry, snub, and exploit—immortal horrors or everlasting splendors.[14]

In other words, everyone will live somewhere forever—either with God in heaven or separated from him in hell. This makes it all the more important that we pursue the knowledge of God while living in a deceived and chaotic culture. Such a pursuit will involve walking with him daily, reflecting his glory to others, and proclaiming the spiritual restoration that is available in Christ, and *only* in Christ, all the while asking God to open spiritually blind eyes and dispel the darkness.

Let us pray for God to send to our nation times of refreshing from his presence (Acts 3:20) and for courage on our part to stand firm in times of testing and to continue proclaiming the truth of his powerful Word. Let us pray that the Holy Spirit will convict people "concerning sin and righteousness and judgment" (John 16:8) so that true spiritual awakening will descend upon our land.

> O Lord, I have heard the report of you, and your work, O Lord, do I fear. In the midst of the years revive it; in the midst of the years make it known; in wrath remember mercy. (Habakkuk 3:2)

Pastor and educator John Guest spoke of the impact George Whitefield's writing had upon him in this regard. Guest read of the *Great Awakening* in Whitefield's journal and gained an understanding of the Holy Spirit's power to change society in a single generation. Guest pointed out that when Whitefield began his ministry, there was deadness in the church to the point that the bishop in London said he did not expect Christianity to survive that generation. Yet as John Guest has written: "Not only was Great Britain radically transformed, but so were the American Colonies—and all through the preaching of the Word of God. It gave me the dream of seeing the same thing in our lifetime."[15]

It is true that we live in a day of mind-boggling change. Just when you thought you had heard it all and can't be surprised anymore, something else pops up. Just when you thought the cultural and political landscape could not get any more insane...well, it just did!

However, in light of God's mighty work in past generations, why would we ever doubt his power to change lives and transform nations today? Why would we not pray fervently in faith for God to send a sweeping awakening to our spiritually needy land?

Furthermore, we have no reason to live defeated lives when the eternal, unchanging, resurrected, victorious Christ is reigning forever and ever. Neither is there any reason to be fearful or anxious when the Bible says that we, as believers, belong to Christ; we are in him, and he is in us. Romans 8:37 says, "In all these things we are more than conquerors through him who loved us."

Years ago, I heard someone say, "*Sent* plus *went* equals *put.*" That is to say, God sends us and in obedience we go. As a result, we will be where God puts us until such time as he moves us, whether geographically or otherwise. The cultural winds of the day won't uproot us.

Therefore, if we are where God sent us, we have every reason to rejoice and no reason to be afraid (see Isaiah 41:10). *Sent* plus *went* equals *put*!

> Is your place a small place?
> Tend it with care!
> He set you there.
>
> Is your place a large place?
> Guard it with care!
> He set you there.
>
> Whate'er your place, it is
> Not yours alone, but His
> Who set you there.[16]

A man who determined to stay in the place where God set him was the great missionary to China, Hudson Taylor. Even in the midst of massive change and upheaval, he stayed. In 1901, he kept getting messages of his missionaries being assassinated by Chinese terrorists. We are told that Taylor's mission had nearly one thousand missionaries in the country, and one by one, they were being killed in the Boxer Rebellion.

From a human perspective, there was nothing Taylor could do about this. However, he could pray, and pray he did! Oh, and one other thing: He sang.

We should do likewise—praying, singing, and resting in God during the hard times as well as the good times. Day after day,

Hudson Taylor's coworkers heard him singing softly the words to his favorite hymn:

> Jesus, I am resting, resting
> In the joy of what Thou art;
> I am finding out the greatness
> Of Thy loving heart.
>
> Thou hast bid me gaze upon Thee,
> And Thy beauty fills my soul,
> For by Thy transforming power,
> Thou hast made me whole.[17]

So whatever your need—whatever the perplexities of the day— keep finding out the greatness of the loving heart of Jesus. Rest in the joy of who he is. Gaze upon him in the Word. Be filled with his beauty. Know his transforming power. And sing! Conditions in our nation and world may go from bad to worse, but you and I can grow ever closer to our heavenly Father and go ever deeper in his living Word.

Thus, as we think about these days of cultural upheaval, it is both insightful and encouraging to read the little book of Habakkuk. If ever a man had reason to be distraught, it would have been the prophet Habakkuk. He saw his own nation overwhelmed by the idolatrous Babylonian forces. However, his book does not end with a funeral dirge; it ends with praise to God!

> Though the fig tree should not blossom, nor fruit be on the vines, the produce of the olive fail and the fields yield no food, the flock be cut off from the fold and there be no herd in the stalls, yet I will rejoice in the Lord; I will take joy in the God of my salvation. God, the Lord, is my strength. (Habakkuk 3:17–19)

In the vernacular of today, I suppose we could say it like this: though the economy collapses, the banks fail, inflation soars, fuel supplies dwindle, store shelves become empty, and unemployment surges...*yet* I will rejoice in the Lord and be glad in the God who is my salvation and strength!

As we have seen throughout this book, the Lord our God is perfect in all his ways and completely trustworthy. What a privilege to bring every need and every opportunity to him! King David declares, "The Lord is a stronghold for the oppressed, a stronghold in times of trouble. And those who know your name put their trust in you, for you, O Lord, have not forsaken those who seek you" (Psalm 9:9–10).

> We may trust Him fully
> All for us to do;
> They who trust Him wholly
> Find Him wholly true.[18]

Therefore, in a day of cultural insanity, let us determine to think rightly *about* God, live boldly *for* God, and trust fully *in* God for in him we have "strong encouragement to hold fast to the hope set before us...a sure and steadfast anchor of the soul" (Hebrews 6:18, 19).

Come what may, our God reigns!

EPILOGUE

For the Generations to Come

When I was in London some years ago, I learned that during the dark days of World War II when bombs were falling on the city, Winston Churchill awoke every morning and immediately asked, "Is it still standing?" Those who heard the question knew exactly what he was asking about. Is St. Paul's Cathedral still standing? Churchill understood that this church building—one of the iconic and architectural wonders of London—held great symbolism for his beleaguered nation.

However, another building—little known in London today, it seems—was not as fortunate as St. Paul's during the war. The Metropolitan Tabernacle (pastored almost a century earlier by Charles Spurgeon) was burned down when it was hit by incendiary bombs in the longest air raid of World War II in May of 1941. Only the front portico and basement survived, and in 1957, the present structure was rebuilt but with a different design.

The attendance at the Tabernacle, however, greatly diminished after the war due to few of the members being able to return to a heavily devastated central London. By 1970, the numbers had further fallen to the point where only a few pews were occupied, but God in his grace began a fresh new work in this historic church. Though the present worship center of the Tabernacle is much smaller than the original building in Spurgeon's day, it is filled each Sunday with people worshipping God and studying his Word. In fact, over the last

175

forty years, large numbers of people have come into the Tabernacle, many professions of faith in Christ have taken place, and a number of vibrant ministries have been established.

Yes, I found Westminster Abbey interesting and the design of St. Paul's Cathedral impressive, but my greater delight was in visiting the Metropolitan Tabernacle. Its beauty is seen not in the rather ordinary building (except for the large portico) but in its amazing legacy and the vibrant ministries still being carried out in central London and beyond. I'm glad St. Paul's Cathedral escaped extensive damage from Hitler's bombs and is still standing (as Churchill so desired), but that which stands at the Metropolitan Tabernacle and other Bible-centered congregations throughout the world is far more than a building of stone, bricks, and mortar. That which stands in those places is a legacy of faithful gospel proclamation and Christ-centered ministry.

Oh, that in our day, we will pursue the knowledge of God, grow daily through his Word, live out a biblical worldview, and proclaim the good news of the gospel with authority, conviction, and joy—all for the glory of God! Our own "beleaguered" nation is in desperate need of a generation doing just that. Furthermore, if we are faithful in this regard, we will be laying an unshakable foundation for the generations to come.

> You yourselves like *living stones* are being built up as a spiritual house, to be a holy priesthood, to offer spiritual sacrifices acceptable to God through Jesus Christ. (1 Peter 2:5, emphasis mine)

Keep standing! *Soli Deo gloria.*

*****

The appendixes at the end of this book are for your guidance and encouragement in pursuing the knowledge of God, increasing in understanding of and love for the gospel, and standing firm against the attacks of Satan.

APPENDIX 1

A Prayer Guide for Spiritual Warfare

Finally, be strong in the Lord and in the strength of his
might. Put on the whole armor of God, that you may
be able to stand against the schemes of the devil.
—Ephesians 6:10–11

The following guide is intended to be a help for putting on the whole armor of God (Ephesians 6:10–18) as a part of beginning your day with him and as a means of successfully resisting Satan's strategies and attacks. There are, of course, other important elements of a devotional time that involve praise (Psalm 95:1–2), reading and meditating on the Word (Psalm 1:2), intercessory prayer (Colossians 1:9–14), and making your own requests known to God (Philippians 4:6–7; 1 John 5:14–15).

The purpose of this particular guide, however, is to provide direction for utilizing the whole armor of God. You may want to incorporate your own words as you pray through the truths presented in this prayer guide. Also, it will be instructive and encouraging to meditate on the Scripture passages that are listed here.

The guide also brings out some of the themes emphasized throughout the previous pages of this book, such as the knowledge of God, the attributes of God, the authority of biblical truth, holiness of life, the primacy of the gospel, and the empowering of the Holy Spirit.

As we put on the whole armor of God, we will be prepared for the spiritual warfare we face every day, and we will be able to live out a biblical worldview in the midst of a hostile and increasingly decadent culture.

Introductory prayer

O Lord, you are my Creator, Redeemer, and heavenly Father—the one true and eternal God, "from whom are all things and for whom we exist" (1 Corinthians 8:6). As Father, Son, and Holy Spirit, you are triune in your being and Lord over all.

Therefore, dear Father, I acknowledge your right to rule over every area of my life at all times. By your grace, I submit to the lordship of Christ.

Please help me offer to you this day the love, praise, devotion, and thanksgiving that are due your glorious name and of which you are infinitely worthy.

> From the rising of the sun to its setting, the
> name of the Lord is to be praised! (Psalm 113:3)

Father, I ask you to fix my heart on you today and keep me in quietness of spirit, trusting in you and resting in your care.

> Let me hear in the morning of your stead-
> fast love for in you I trust. Make me know the
> way I should go for to you I lift up my soul.
> (Psalm 143:8)

Please keep me strong in you, O Lord, and give me your perfect guidance as I put on the whole armor of God.

Belt of truth

"Stand therefore, having fastened on the belt of truth" (Ephesians 6:14).

Father, I confess your Word as absolute truth and acknowledge it as the belt of truth, given for my instruction and for my victory in spiritual warfare.

Thank you for the precious gift of your Word. I ask you to implant it deeply within me today as I read and meditate upon it so that I may grow in the knowledge of God and bring glory to you.

> Teach me your way, O Lord, that I may walk in your truth; unite my heart to fear your name. (Psalm 86:11)

Father, I ask you for opportunities to communicate your Word to others through any channels of your sovereign choosing. I also ask you to keep me usable and to protect me from sin so that my life will be pleasing to you and that I will be able to proclaim the gospel to others in the power of the Holy Spirit and for your glory alone.

Breastplate of righteousness

"And having put on the breastplate of righteousness" (Ephesians 6:14).

Dear Father, I acknowledge the breastplate of righteousness. Thank you for the finished work of Christ and for your own perfect righteousness that you have given me in him through his atoning death on my behalf (see 2 Corinthians 5:21; 1 Peter 2:24). I rejoice in this wondrous grace, O Lord, and in the assurance it gives me that I am not defined by sin nor under its control.

Therefore, I present myself to you as one who has been brought from death to life and the members of my body to you as instruments for righteousness (based on Romans 6:13).

Father, I ask you to keep me fully alert to the earliest and most insidious approaches of temptation today and give me the grace and power to resist all attacks of the devil so that I may live in holiness and honor (see James 4:7). I ask you to protect my mind and emotions and empower me to overcome spiritual oppression, especially in the following areas.

- Fear
- Anxiety
- Discouragement
- Depression
- Anger
- Bitterness
- Pride
- Self-centeredness
- Lustful desires
- Discontentment
- Unnecessary stress
- Harmful and needless distraction
- Others: _____

Thank you, Father, for your all-sufficient protection and for your perfect guidance (see Psalm 32:8). Please help me fill my mind today with that which is true, honorable, just, pure, lovely, and commendable—that I may dwell on these things (based on Philippians 4:8, CSB).

Help me cleanse myself, I pray, "from every defilement of body and spirit, bringing holiness to completion in the fear of God" (2 Corinthians 7:1).

Shoes of peace

"And, as shoes for your feet, having put on the readiness given by the gospel of peace" (Ephesians 6:15).

Father, I joyfully acknowledge the gospel of peace and thank you for the peace you have given me through Jesus my Lord.

> Therefore, since we have been justified by faith, we have peace with God through our Lord Jesus Christ. (Romans 5:1)

I also thank you that I can stand firm in the midst of spiritual warfare because of the shoes of the gospel of peace. Please help me to so stand this day (see Romans 8:31).

> You keep him in perfect peace whose mind
> is stayed on you, because he trusts in you. (Isaiah
> 26:3)

O Lord, I ask you to increase my understanding of the gospel and my love for it by taking me deeper into its glories. Please give me the desire, the readiness, and the open doors to make the gospel known.

> For I am not ashamed of the gospel, for it is
> the power of God for salvation to everyone who
> believes. (Romans 1:16)

Shield of faith

"In all circumstances take up the shield of faith, with which you can extinguish all the flaming darts of the evil one" (Ephesians 6:16).

I take up the shield of faith, dear Father, that I may be able to extinguish all the flaming darts of the evil one. I confess that you are my shelter, stronghold, and everlasting rock (see Psalm 91:1, 27:1; Isaiah 26:4).

> You are a hiding place for me; you preserve
> me from trouble; you surround me with shouts of
> deliverance. (Psalm 32:7)

Thank you, O Lord, for being my protection against the attacks of Satan and for making me more than a conqueror through Christ who loved me (see Romans 8:37; Psalm 18:1–3).

Please help me walk by faith in you throughout this day. You are "my God, in whom I trust" (Psalm 91:2; see also Proverbs 3:5–6).

Helmet of salvation

"And take the helmet of salvation" (Ephesians 6:17).

Father, I take up the helmet of salvation and acknowledge with gladness that you who began a good work in me will bring it to completion at the day of Jesus Christ (see Philippians 1:6). Thank you for this glorious promise and the assurance it gives me of my eternal salvation and of your faithful, continuing work in my life.

Therefore, O Lord, I ask that your presence be so real to me today that my first thought in everything will be to do your will and to avoid whatever would bring you sorrow (see 1 John 2:15–17; see also 1 Thessalonians 5:21–22).

Thank you, Father, for your promise of a full and final salvation to come—an eternal and glorious future I have in Christ because of "the hope of salvation" (1 Thessalonians 5:8). I joyfully acknowledge that this hope is guaranteed by the resurrection of Jesus from the dead.

Therefore, I thank you, O Lord, that he who finished his work *for* me will also finish his work *in* me.

Sword of the Spirit

"And take...the sword of the Spirit, which is the Word of God" (Ephesians 6:17).

Father, I take up the sword of the Spirit and confess it as your living Word—infinitely powerful to defeat all of Satan's attacks. I ask you for wisdom and guidance in understanding the Word today.

I also ask, O Lord, that you empower me to use it as the sword of the Spirit to overcome the temptations of the world, the flesh, and the devil (see 1 John 2:15–17).

I thank you that the Holy Spirit gives a word from the Scriptures that speaks to the immediate need in my life. Please make known to me that word and help me to readily and properly apply it.

Father, I desire to be filled with the Holy Spirit. Therefore, by your grace, I joyfully submit to this glorious filling (see Ephesians 5:18). I ask that you empower me to walk by the Spirit today so that I "will not gratify the desires of the flesh" (Galatians 5:16; see also Romans 8:5–6, 13:14).

Concluding petitions

O Lord, I thank you for this day and accept it as a gift from you. Please help me use it for your purposes and for your glory alone (see Ephesians 5:15–16).

I pray that you will lead me to know when to speak and when to be silent, when to act and when not to act, so that I may do your will at all times.

Father, I ask you for spiritual, emotional, and physical health. I also ask you for the strength, initiative, and mental clarity I need to accomplish the work today that is a part of your sovereign calling upon my life.

O Lord, I acknowledge and thank you that you give power to the faint and to him who has no might you increase strength (based on Isaiah 40:29). I gladly confess that your grace is sufficient for me for your power "is made perfect in weakness." Therefore, "when I am weak, then I am strong" (2 Corinthians 12:9–10).

To you, my triune God, be all the glory for the victory you give me in spiritual warfare. All this I pray in the mighty, majestic, and holy name of the Lord Jesus Christ. Amen.

APPENDIX 2

Building Your Life upon the Gospel

We have an enemy who is at war with us. The devil can no longer claim us as his own, but he can try to do the next best (worst) thing—and that is to lead us astray and render us ineffective witnesses for Christ.

Therefore, in addition to putting on the whole armor of God, it is important that we also employ the discipline of preaching the gospel to ourselves. This will greatly encourage and stabilize us in our battle against the devil and will give us an ever-increasing awareness of the beauty and depth of the gospel itself.

We know, of course, how important it is to share the gospel with those who do not know Christ. Yet it is easy to think in terms of the gospel being only for the unsaved. That is to say, the gospel is only a door a person walks through to become a Christian. Then, once that happens, he or she doesn't really need the gospel anymore except to share it with people who are still outside the door. However, that is a tragic misconception. The gospel is also for Christians.

For example, the apostle Paul writes, "I am eager to preach the gospel to you also who are in Rome" (Romans 1:15). Paul is writing to believers here, a fact that the previous verses in Romans 1 make clear. He understood (as we must understand as well) "that the unsaved need the gospel in order to come to know Christ, while the saved need the gospel in order to become more like Christ."[1]

Paul was also writing to believers when he said, "Now I would remind you, brothers, of the gospel I preached to you, which you received, in which you stand" (1 Corinthians 15:1). Thus, to properly stand in the gospel, we must stay constantly focused upon it, which means we keep studying it and faithfully declaring it to ourselves. C. J. Mahaney has written: "Reminding ourselves of the gospel is the most important daily habit we can establish."[2]

Furthermore, the Bible says, "Faith comes from hearing, and hearing through the word of Christ" (Romans 10:17) or literally "the message about Christ." Therefore, it stands to reason that if faith comes from hearing the gospel, then we need to hear it throughout our lives because we want our faith to keep growing as long as we live. In order for this to happen, we must keep going deeper into the heart of the gospel itself. It has been said that we can never go *beyond* the gospel, but we can always go *deeper* in the gospel.

Thus, as Christians, we preach the gospel to ourselves every day by calling to mind the atoning sacrifice of Christ on our behalf— the result of which has provided us forgiveness, eternal life, and the assurance of a future in which we will reign with Christ forever! Could any reality be more thrilling?

So preach this truth to your own soul. Preach it every day for every day we live should be governed by the truth of the gospel. We have a powerful example in Psalm 42 of the psalmist preaching to himself. He says, "Why are you cast down, O my soul, and why are you in turmoil within me? Hope in God; for I shall again praise him, my salvation and my God" (Psalm 42:5).

Think of it: the biblical writer told his soul what to do—*hope in God*. In the midst of deep despair, the psalmist knew the utmost importance of remembering who God is ("my salvation and my God"). Likewise, we should preach this message to our own souls for the glorious hope of which the psalmist wrote is ultimately fulfilled in Christ. The apostle Paul declares, "For God, who said, 'Let light shine out of darkness,' has shone in our hearts to give the light of the knowledge of the glory of God in the face of Jesus Christ" (2 Corinthians 4:6).

Therefore, a daily focus on God and the glorious gospel of his Son will yield supremely powerful encouragement for these perilous times in which we live. Moreover, preaching the gospel to yourself will involve the following:

Gospel-centered knowledge

The writer prays in Psalm 119:11, "I have stored up your word in my heart that I might not sin against you." The psalmist understood the great importance of treasuring God's Word and storing it up in his heart for it is only in doing so that believers can be daily instructed, encouraged, and strengthened by it.

Therefore, consider memorizing key passages of Scripture that define and describe the gospel such as Isaiah 53:3–6; John 1:12–13; Romans 1:16, 3:23–24, 5:8–9, 8:31–34; 1 Corinthians 15:1–4; 2 Corinthians 5:21; Ephesians 2:8–9; and Titus 3:4–7. Since God wants his Word in our hearts, it stands to reason that he will help us with committing it to memory if we ask him.

Furthermore, if we are growing in our knowledge of God's Word, we will be brought nearer to Jesus and his cross in ever-increasing ways. In fact, wherever you are in your Bible reading, seek to identify how each passage relates to the death of Christ and its eternal significance. It's been said that every passage of Scripture in both the Old and New Testaments either predicts, prepares for, reflects, or results from the finished work of Christ!

John Stott has said that "the essence of sin is man substituting himself for God, while the essence of salvation is God substituting himself for man."[3] Ponder the amazing significance of 2 Corinthians 5:21 as it speaks to the atonement of Christ on the cross: "For our sake he made him to be sin who knew no sin, so that in him we might become the righteousness of God."

Thus, because our sins are charged to Christ's account and his righteousness credited to us, we are as acceptable in God's sight as is the Son of God himself (see Ephesians 1:4–6). What a staggering truth! Think of it: in Christ, we have the same standing before God as Jesus has before him. How could there ever be any greater security than this or any better basis for overflowing joy?

Therefore, seek to continually deepen your knowledge of the gospel. Careful reading and study of books like Romans and Galatians will be of immense help in this regard.

Gospel-centered remembrance

We certainly do not want to dwell on the past or be controlled by it. However, there is a proper way to remember it, and that's by allowing the past to remind us of the transforming power of the gospel in our lives.

This was certainly the desire of the apostle Paul. He says, "Formerly I was a blasphemer, persecutor, and insolent opponent. But I received mercy because I had acted ignorantly in unbelief" (1 Timothy 1:13). Although these words were penned many years after Paul's conversion, he clearly remembered his many sins before meeting the risen Christ on the road to Damascus. Obviously, Paul was not controlled by his past, but he was committed to remembering what he once was because to do so was to be overjoyed by the stunning grace and complete forgiveness of God.

Therefore, take time to daily reflect upon the change God has brought in your own life due to the death of his Son on your behalf. Always keep the cross central!

If you've not already done so, consider writing out your testimony in a few paragraphs. This can be a very encouraging and helpful project in terms of calling to mind how the gospel has changed you. Furthermore, it will help you be ready to share with others the spiritual transformation you have experienced.

Be sure your testimony is very specific as you show the true nature of the gospel. Write about how you were separated from God and under condemnation but then explain that you were born again (John 3:1–8) when God brought you to repentance and faith in Christ alone as your Lord and Savior.

Be careful not to overstress the past but rather emphasize your life now as a result of the extraordinary power of the gospel.

Gospel-centered prayer

Through the death and resurrection of Jesus Christ, we are able to approach God in prayer at any time day or night. The writer of Hebrews says that "we have confidence to enter the holy places by the blood of Jesus" and, therefore, should "draw near with a true heart in full assurance of faith" (Hebrews 10:19, 22). What a marvelous privilege then to pray with this full assurance because of the truth of the gospel: Jesus has paid our sin debt in its entirety and has thus given us complete access to God! Let's consider then the elements involved in gospel-centered prayer.

First, begin by thanking God for the willing sacrifice of Jesus on the cross whereby he bore God's wrath for sin on your behalf, rose from the dead, and won over Satan for time and eternity. Nothing in our topsy-turvy, ever-changing culture can diminish the glorious truth of Christ's atonement; consequently, believers will never be separated from the love of God (Romans 8:38–39)! Also, thank God that you have been given the Holy Spirit to dwell within you, lead you into the truth, assure you of your eternal salvation, bring forth spiritual fruit in your life, and empower you to live every day for the glory of God.

Secondly, ask God to enable you to know and obey his Word so that you may delight in it, meditate on it, be changed by it, and glorify him through it. In this way, you will be able to truly pursue the knowledge of God and gain deeper understanding of gospel truth.

Thirdly, pray that God will open doors for you to share his Word with others. It is only as more and more people are brought out of spiritual darkness into the light of the life-changing gospel of Jesus Christ that lasting change will come about in our nation and world. Thus, in true Trinitarian fashion, ask the Father for a heart that believes him to reveal the Son, through the power of the Spirit, in ever-increasing ways to ever-increasing numbers of people through an ever-increasing army of witnesses who proclaim the good news!

Fourthly, determine to intercede for your brothers and sisters in Christ on the basis of the apostle Paul's exhortation to the Thessalonian believers:

> But we ought always to give thanks to God for you, brothers beloved by the Lord, because God chose you as the firstfruits to be saved, through sanctification by the Spirit and belief in the truth. To this he called you through our gospel, so that you may obtain the glory of our Lord Jesus Christ. So then, brothers, stand firm and hold to the traditions that you were taught by us, either by our spoken word or by our letter. Now may our Lord Jesus Christ himself, and God our Father, who loved us and gave us eternal comfort and good hope through grace, comfort your hearts and establish them in every good work and word. (2 Thessalonians 2:13–17; see also Ephesians 1:16–19 and Colossians 1:9–12)

Always remember, our entering into the presence of God the Father is only through God the Son and his finished work on the cross. Therefore, the truth of the gospel should form the basis and heart of our prayers.

So pray the gospel. Pray it every day.

Gospel-centered worship

The daily intake of gospel truth should always result in the exuberant worship of God himself. *Theology* leads to *doxology*. In fact, we learn in the book of Revelation that all of history culminates in believers from all the ages worshipping God for all eternity! It is clear then that worship is of the utmost importance. In fact, "the supreme reason for human existence is to worship God for his love, greatness and saving deeds."[4]

Yes, we were created to be worshippers of the living God. Thus, the singular motive of worship is to bring glory and pleasure to him; worship is for God and for him alone. Therefore, when we worship, we are fulfilling the very purpose for which we were made!

Furthermore, one of the ways we engage in gospel-centered worship is through singing about the cross. Now at this point, I am not primarily referring to congregational singing though that is of great importance. Rather, I'm talking about singing in our personal devotional times. You don't have to be able to read music or have a good singing voice in order to sing. After all, it's not the quality of your voice; it's the condition of your heart that makes the difference. If we have a heart for worship, we will want to sing praise to God. David prayed, "I will be glad and exult in you; I will sing praise to your name, O Most High" (Psalm 9:2). It is indeed an incalculable joy and privilege to sing the glorious gospel of Jesus Christ!

Moreover, it is important to choose hymns and songs that are scripturally sound and are clearly centered on magnifying Jesus and what he has done to purchase our salvation. As examples, consider using the following hymns:

- "My Jesus, I Love Thee"
- "When I Survey the Wondrous Cross"
- "Hallelujah, What a Savior!"
- "I Will Sing of My Redeemer"
- "Alas! And Did My Savior Bleed?"
- "Come Behold the Wondrous Mystery"
- "How Rich a Treasure We Possess"
- "And Can It Be?"
- "In Christ Alone"
- "Before the Throne of God Above"
- "How Deep the Father's Love for Us"
- "Sacred Head, Now Wounded"
- "In the Cross Alone I Glory"

These hymns, and many others like them, focus on the cross and will take you deep into the suffering of our Lord and the *mean-*

ing of those sufferings. Therefore, it is very important to ponder carefully the words of the hymns and songs you sing and allow them to lead you into worship.

In conclusion, always remember that each time you engage the gospel in any of the aforementioned ways, you must ask God to open your eyes through the power of the Holy Spirit so that you may see the gospel in its fullness. It is a blessing to pray the words of the psalmist, "Open my eyes, that I may behold wondrous things out of your law" (Psalm 119:18).

Furthermore, God has not only provided perfect security in Christ so that we need never fear separation from him in hell, but God also protects his children from the daily assaults of Satan. However, the gospel must be the very center of all you and I do.

Rejoice then that God has called and empowered believers to love the gospel deeply, know it thoroughly, rejoice in it constantly, and proclaim it faithfully—all in the power of the Holy Spirit for the glory of God alone and for the advancement of his kingdom.

Therefore, call to mind every day in one form or another the good news of the Bible that Jesus died vicariously on the cross and rose victoriously from the dead. This is the message of the gospel; it never gets old, and we should fervently preach it to ourselves. As Martin Luther reportedly declared, "We need to hear the gospel every day because we forget it every day."

It is also important to remind ourselves that Jesus ascended back to his Father in heaven in a glorified body where he sovereignly reigns. Furthermore, he will return to judge sinners, right all wrongs, and establish his glorious kingdom forever in which those redeemed by his blood will reign with him for eternity.

The late Timothy Keller wrote these moving words:

> The gospel is this: We are more sinful and flawed in ourselves than we ever dared believe, yet at the very same time we are more loved and accepted in Jesus Christ than we ever dared hope.[5]

Indeed, this is the glorious truth of the gospel, and it is why we build our lives upon it.

> Full atonement! Can it be?
> Hallelujah, what a Savior![6]

APPENDIX 3

Resources for Further Reading

The following resources are based on the three main sections of this book and are recommended for further reading and study. Additional resources are also listed for studies on culture and worldview.

Chapter 1: Seeing...but *Not* Seeing (God Revealed in Nature)

- Blanchard, John. *Does God Believe in Atheists?* Auburn, MA: Evangelical Press, 2000.
- Boa, Kenneth D., and Robert M. Bowman Jr. *20 Compelling Evidences that God Exists: Discover Why Believing in God Makes So Much Sense.* Tulsa OK: RiverOak Publishing, a division of Cook Communication Ministries, 2002.
- McDowell, Josh D., and Thomas Williams. *How to Know God Exists: Solid Reasons to Believe in God, Discover Truth, and Find Meaning in Your Life.* Carol Stream, IL: Tyndale Momentum, 2022.
- Simmons III, Richard E. *Reflections on the Existence of God: A Series of Essays.* Birmingham, AL: Union Hill Publishing, 2019.
- Sproul, Robert Charles. *Does God Exist?* Sanford, FL: Ligonier Ministries, 2019.

Chapter 2: Into the Courtroom (God Revealed through His Word)

- DeYoung, Kevin. *Taking God at His Word: Why the Bible Is Knowable, Necessary, and Enough, and What That Means for You and Me.* Wheaton, IL: Crossway, 2014.
- Edwards, Brian H. *Nothing but the Truth: The inspiration, Authority and History of the Bible Explained.* Webster, NY: Evangelical Press, 2006.
- Kistler, Don, ed. *Sola Scriptura.* Sanford, FL: Reformation Trust Publishing, 2009.
- Lutzer, Erwin W. *Seven Reasons Why You Can Trust the Bible.* Chicago, IL: Moody Press, 1998.
- Plummer, Robert L. *The Story of Scripture: How We Got Our Bible and Why We Can Trust It.* Grand Rapids, MI: Kregel Publications, 2013.
- Stott, John R. W. *You Can Trust the Bible: Our Foundation for Belief and Obedience.* Grand Rapids, MI: Discovery House Publishers edition, 1991.
- Thomas, Derek W. H. *The Bible: God's Inerrant Word.* Carlisle, PA: The Banner of Truth Trust, 2018.

Chapters 3 and 4: Pondering the Imponderable (The Attributes of God)

- Beeke, Joel R., and Brian Cosby. *None Else: 31 Meditations on God's Character and Attributes.* Grand Rapids, MI: Reformation Heritage Books, 2020.
- Jones, Mark. *God Is: A Devotional Guide to the Attributes of God.* Wheaton, IL: Crossway, 2017.
- Lawson, Steven J. *Show Me Your Glory: Understanding the Majestic Splendor of God.* Orlando, FL: Reformation Trust Publishing, 2020.
- Packer, J. I. *Knowing God.* Downers Grove, IL: InterVarsity Press, 1973, 2021.
- Pink, Arthur W. *The Nature of God.* Chicago, IL: Moody Press, 1975, 1999.

- Ryken, Philip Graham. *Discovering God: In Stories from the Bible*. Phillipsburg, NJ: P&R Publishing, 1999.
- Tozer, A. W. *The Knowledge of the Holy* included in *A. W. Tozer, Three Spiritual Classics in One Volume*. Chicago, IL: Moody Publishers, 1961, 2018.

Chapter 5: Promises Too Good to Be True…If Made by Anyone but God! (The Promises of God)

- Alleine, Joseph. *Precious Promises*. Carlisle, PA: The Banner of Truth Trust, 2021.
- Beeke, Joel R., and James A. La Belle. *Living by God's Promises*. Grand Rapids, MI: Reformation Heritage Books, 2010.
- Piper, John. *Future Grace: The Purifying Power of the Promises of God*. Colorado Springs, CO: Multnomah Books, Revised, 2012.
- Sproul, Robert Charles. *The Promises of God: Discovering the One Who Keeps His Word*. Colorado Springs, CO: David C. Cook, 2013.
- Spurgeon, Charles Haddon. *The Promises of God: A New Edition of the Classic Devotional Based on the English Standard Version*, edited by Tim Chester. Wheaton, IL: Crossway, 2019.

Chapter 6: Correctly Fearing God

- Bridges, Jerry. *The Joy of Fearing God*. Colorado Springs, CO: Waterbrook Press, 1997.
- Fox, Christina. *A Holy Fear: Trading Lesser Fears for the Fear of the Lord*. Grand Rapids, MI: Reformation Heritage Books, 2020.
- Martin, Albert N. *The Forgotten Fear: Where Have All the God-Fearers Gone?* Grand Rapids, MI: Reformation Heritage Books, 2015.

- Reeves, Michael. *Rejoice and Tremble: The Surprising Good News of the Fear of the Lord.* Wheaton, IL: Crossway, 2021.

Chapter 7: Correctly Bearing God's Image

- Darling, Daniel. *The Dignity Revolution: Reclaiming God's Rich Vision for Humanity.* United Kingdom: The Good Book Company, 2018.
- Hedges, Brian G. *The Story of His Glory.* Wheaton, IL: Crossway, 2019.
- Sproul, Robert Charles. *The Hunger for Significance: Seeing the Image of God in Man.* Phillipsburg, NJ: P&R Publishing, Third Edition, 2020.
- Sunshine, Glenn, and Timothy D. Padgett. *The Image Restored: The Imago Dei and Creation.* Colorado Springs, CO: Colson Press, 2021.
- Wilkin, Jen. *In His Image: 10 Ways God Calls Us to Reflect His Character.* Wheaton, IL: Crossway, 2018.

Other Resources for Culture and Worldview Studies

- Baucham, Voddie T. *The Ever-Loving Truth: Can Faith Thrive in a Post-Christian Culture?* Washington, DC: Salem Books, 2004, 2023.
- Beeke, Joel R., ed. *The Beauty and Glory of the Christian Worldview.* Grand Rapids, MI: Reformation Heritage Books, 2017.
- Colson, Charles W., and Nancy Pearcey. *How Now Shall We Live?* Wheaton, IL: Tyndale House Publishers, 1999.
- Guinness, Os. *Renaissance: The Power of the Gospel However Dark the Times.* Downers Grove, IL: InterVarsity Press, 2014.
- Koukl, Gregory. *Street Smarts: Using Questions to Answer Christianity's Toughest Challenges.* Grand Rapids, MI: Zondervan Reflective, 2023.

- Lennox, John C. *2084: Artificial Intelligence and the Future of Humanity*. Grand Rapids, MI: Zondervan Reflective, 2020.
- Lutzer, Erwin W. *No Reason to Hide: Standing for Christ in a Collapsing Culture*. Eugene, OR: Harvest House Publishers, 2022.
- MacArthur, John, and Nathan Busenitz, general editors. *Right Thinking for a Culture in Chaos: Responding Biblically to Today's Most Urgent Needs*. Eugene, OR: Harvest House Publishers, 2023.
- Metaxas, Eric. *Letter to the American Church*. Washington, DC: Salem Books, 2022.
- Mohler, R. Albert Jr. *The Gathering Storm: Secularism, Culture, and the Church*. Nashville, TN: Nelson Books, an imprint of Thomas Nelson, 2020.
- Myers, Jeff. *The Secret Battle of Ideas About God: Overcoming the Outbreak of Five Fatal Worldviews*. Colorado Springs, CO: David C Cook, 2017.
- Myers, Jeff. *Understanding the Culture: A Survey of Social Engagement*. Manitou Springs, CO: Summit Ministries, in cooperation with David C Cook, 2017.
- Pearcey, Nancy. *Total Truth: Liberating Christianity from Its Cultural Captivity*. Wheaton, IL: Crossway, 2004, 2005.
- Stonestreet, John, and Brett Kunkle. *A Practical Guide to Culture: Helping the Next Generation Navigate Today's World*. Colorado Springs, CO: David C Cook, 2017, 2020.
- Wells, David F. *God in the Whirlwind: How the Holy-Love of God Reorients Our World*. Wheaton, IL: Crossway, 2014.

NOTES

Introduction: What God Is Doing

1   John Stonestreet and Brett Kunkle, *A Practical Guide to Culture: Helping the Next Generation Navigate Today's World* (Colorado Springs, CO: David C. Cook, 2017), 18.

2   From a letter by John MacArthur to *Grace to You* supporters, January 19, 2021.

3   J. I. Packer, *Hot Tub Religion* (Wheaton, IL: Tyndale House Publishers, 1987), 32.

4   Charles W. Colson, *How Now Shall We Live?* (Wheaton, IL: Tyndale House Publishers, 1999), 17.

5   Ibid., 100.

Chapter 1: Seeing...but *Not* Seeing

1   W. A. Criswell, cited in Ray Pritchard, *Green Pastures, Quiet Waters: Refreshing Moments from the Psalms* (Chicago, IL: Moody Press, 1999), 61.

2   Hank Hanegraaff, *The Creation Answer Book* (Nashville, TN: Thomas Nelson, 2012), 17.

3   Kenneth D. Boa and Robert M. Bowman Jr., *20 Compelling Evidences That God Exists: Discover Why Believing in God Makes So Much Sense* (Tulsa, OK: RiverOak Publishing, 2002), 47.

4   Frederick Talbott, *Churchill on Courage: Timeless Wisdom for Persevering* (Nashville, TN: Thomas Nelson, 1996).

5   Ralph Earle, *Word Meanings in the New Testament: One Volume Edition* (Grand Rapids, MI: Baker Book House, 1986), 138.

6   Jonathan Wells, cited in Charlie H. Campbell, *One-Minute Answers to Skeptics: Concise Responses to the Top 40 Questions* (Eugene, OR: Harvest House Publishers, 2005/2010), 76.

7   Jeremiah J. Johnston, *Unimaginable: What Our World Would Be Like Without Christianity* (Minneapolis, MN: Bethany House Publishers, 2017), 29.

8   Thomas Brooks, cited in Tim Challies, *Words from the Wise: Knowing and Enjoying God* (Eugene, OR: Harvest House Publishers, 2021), 16.

9   Roy B. Zuck, *The Speaker's Quote Book* (Grand Rapids, MI: Kregel Publications, 2009), 174.

10 R. C. Sproul, *Not A Chance: God, Science, and the Revolt against Reason* (Grand Rapids, MI: Baker Books, 2014), 22.

11 Paul Enns, *Approaching God: Daily Readings in Systematic Theology* (Chicago, IL: Moody Press, 1991), January 3 reading.

12 Frederick Hoyle, cited in Nathan Busenitz, *Reasons We Believe: 50 Lines of Evidence that Confirm the Christian Faith* (Wheaton, IL: Crossway Books, 2008), 46.

13 John Stonestreet, *Breakpoint Daily* (Colorado Springs, CO: The Colson Center for Christian Worldview, January 25, 2023).

14 Chesterton, *Breakpoint Daily*.

15 Woody Allen, cited in Gyles Brandreth, ed., *Oxford Dictionary of Humorous Quotations*, Fifth Edition (Oxford, UK: Oxford University Press, 2013), 51.

16 John MacArthur, *The MacArthur New Testament Commentary: Romans 1–8* (Chicago, IL: Moody Press, 1991), 103.

17 G. K. Chesterton, cited in Charles Colson, *How Now Shall We Live? Devotional* (Wheaton, IL: Tyndale House Publishers, 2004), 264.

18 Václav Havel, cited in Philip Graham Ryken, *Discovering God: In Stories from the Bible* (Phillipsburg, NJ: P&R Publishing, 1999), 176.

19 Eric Metaxas, *Letter to the American Church* (Washington, DC: Salem Books, 2022), xi.

20 C. S. Lewis, cited in Stephen J. Nichols, *Welcome to the Story: Reading, Loving, and Living God's Word* (Wheaton, IL: Crossway, 2011), 105.

Chapter 2: Into the Courtroom

1 John MacArthur, foreword in Nathan Busenitz, *Reasons We Believe: 50 Lines of Evidence that Confirm the Christian Faith* (Wheaton, IL: Crossway Books, 2008), 13.

2 Cited in Bill Brown, Breakpoint.org, *Stephen Hawking's Accidental Apologetic* (Colorado Springs, CO: The Colson Center for Christian Worldview, February 28, 2019), 3.

3 Ibid., 2.

4 Ibid., 3.

5 John MacArthur, *The Battle for the Beginning: The Bible on Creation and the Fall of Adam* (Nashville, TN: Thomas Nelson, 2001), 41.

6 Ibid.

7 *CSB Holy Land Illustrated Bible* (Nashville, TN: Holman Bible Publishers, 2020), 1490.

8 Nelson Glueck, cited in John Blanchard, *How to Enjoy Your Bible* (Webster, NY: Evangelical Press, 2007), 53.

9 John Elder, cited in Don Stewart, *10 Reasons to Trust the Bible* (Santa Ana, CA: AskDon Publishers, 1990, revised and enlarged 2009), 59.

10 Ibid., 38.

11 A. Z. Conrad, cited in George H. Guthrie, *Read the Bible for Life: Understanding & Living God's Word* (Nashville, TN: B&H Publishing Group, 2011), 4.

[12] This account told by David Jeremiah, *Sanctuary: Finding Moments of Refuge in the Presence of God* (Nashville, TN: Thomas Nelson, 2002), 143.

[13] R. Kent Hughes, *1001 Great Stories and "Quotes"* (Wheaton, IL: Tyndale House, 1998), 313.

[14] John Blanchard, *Why Believe the Bible?* (Wyoming, MI: Evangelical Press, 2004, 2016), 47.

[15] Charles W. Colson, *Loving God* (Grand Rapids, MI: Zondervan Publishing House, 1987), 55.

[16] Robert J. Morgan, *Nelson's Complete Book of Stories, Illustrations, and Quotes* (Nashville, TN: Thomas Nelson, 2000), 55.

[17] Paul Enns, *The Moody Handbook of Theology: Revised and Expanded* (Chicago, IL: Moody Publishers, 2014), 164.

[18] Brian Edwards, *Nothing but the Truth: The Inspiration, Authority and History of the Bible Explained* (Webster, NY: Evangelical Press, 2006), 139.

[19] J. C. Ryle, *Practical Religion: Being Plain Papers on the Daily Duties, Experience, Dangers, and Privileges of Professing Christians* (Carlisle, PA: The Banner of Truth Trust, 2013, first published, 1878), 136.

[20] This story told in R. Kent Hughes, *1001 Great Stories and "Quotes"* (Wheaton, IL: Tyndale House, 1998), 29.

[21] Vance Havner, *The Vance Havner Notebook*, compiled by Dennis J. Hester (Grand Rapids, MI: Baker Book House, 1989), 219.

[22] Ignatius of Antioch, *NIV Archeological Study Bible* (Grand Rapids, MI: Zondervan, 2005), 2028.

[23] Robert Chapman, cited in Erwin Lutzer, *Seven Reasons Why You Can Trust the Bible* (Chicago, IL: Moody Press, 1998), 31–32.

Chapter 3: Pondering the Imponderable (1)

[1] This account cited in Steven J. Lawson, *Show Me Your Glory: Understanding the Majestic Splendor of God* (Orlando, FL: Reformation Trust Publishing, 2020), 3.

[2] Charles Spurgeon, cited in Peter Jeffery, *Bitesize Theology* (Webster, NY: Evangelical Press, 2000), 20–21.

[3] Aiden Wilson Tozer, *The Knowledge of the Holy* included in *A. W. Tozer, Three Spiritual Classics in One Volume* (Chicago, IL: Moody Publishers, 1961, 2018), 13.

[4] John Piper, *The Pleasures of God: Meditations on God's Delight in Being God* (Colorado Springs, CO: Multnomah Books, revised edition 2012), xv.

[5] Ken Gire, cited in Daniel Henderson, *Transforming Prayer: How Everything Changes When You Seek God's Face* (Minneapolis, MN: Bethany House Publishers, 2011), 57.

[6] Christopher J. H. Wright, *Hearing the Message of Daniel: Sustaining Faith in Today's World* (Grand Rapids, MI: Zondervan, Langham Partnership International, 2017), 57.

7   Ibid., 58.

8   Attributed to Martin Luther, cited in Keith and Kristyn Getty, *Sing! How Worship Transforms Your Life, Family, and Church* (Nashville, TN: B&H Publishing Group, 2017), xxiii.

9   Isaac Watts, "We're Marching to Zion."

10 Cited in Jonathan Gibson, *Be Thou My Vision: A Liturgy for Daily Worship* (Wheaton, IL: Crossway, 2021), 233, 235.

11 Augustine, cited in Peter Jeffery, *Bitesize Theology* (Webster NY: Evangelical Press, 2000), 33.

12 Sam Storms, *Tough Topics 2: Biblical Answers to 25 Challenging Questions* (UK: Christian Focus Publications, 2015), 16.

13 Stuart Olyott, cited in Peter Jeffery, *Bitesize Theology* (Webster NY: Evangelical Press, 2000), 36.

14 Bruce Milne, cited in John Blanchard, *Does God Believe in Atheists?* (Darlington, England: Evangelical Press, 2000), 451.

15 Christian George, *Godology: Because Knowing God Changes Everything* (Chicago, IL: Moody Publishers, 2009), 19.

16 Norman Geisler, *Systematic Theology, Volume 2: God, Creation* (Bloomington, MN: Bethany House Publishers, 2003), 293.

17 Sam Storm, *Tough Topics 2*, 15.

18 "Come, Thou Almighty King," Anonymous, circa 1757.

19 Gene Edwards, *The Highest Life: Living with the Indwelling Lord* (Carol Stream, IL: Tyndale House Publishers, 1993), xii.

20 Rick Cornish, *5 Minute Apologist: Maximum Truth in Minimum Time* (Colorado Springs, CO: NavPress, 2005), 119.

21 Cited in Warren W. Wiersbe and Lloyd M. Perry, *The Wycliffe Handbook of Preaching and Preachers* (Chicago, IL: Moody Press, 1984), 189.

22 Arthur W. Pink, *The Attributes of God* (Grand Rapids, MI: Baker Books 1975, new edition 2006), 47.

23 This story cited in R. Kent Hughes, *1001 Great Stories and "Quotes"* (Wheaton, IL: Tyndale House, 1998), 411–412.

24 Stephen Charnock, *The Existence and Attributes of God* (Ann Arbor, MI: Banner of Truth, 1958), 79.

25 Henry F. Lyte "Abide with Me," 1847.

26 Arthur W. Pink, *The Attributes of God*, 41.

27 Isaac Watts, "I Sing the Mighty Power of God," 1715.

28 Edward Mote, "The Solid Rock," 1834.

29 Elliot Clark, cited in Randy Alcorn, *It's All About Jesus: A Treasury of Insights on Our Savior, Lord, and Friend* (Eugene, OR: Harvest House Publishers, 2020), 273–274.

30 Augustus Toplady, cited in Geoffrey Thomas, *You Could Have It All* (Grand Rapids, MI: Reformation Heritage Books, 2020), 54.

31 Maltbie D. Babcock, "This Is My Father's World," 1901.

[32] Scotty Smith and Michael Card, *Unveiled Hope: Eternal Encouragement from the Book of Revelation* (Nashville, TN: Thomas Nelson Publishers, 1997), 70–71.

[33] Christian George, *Godology*, 40.

[34] Arthur W. Pink, *The Attributes of God*, 40.

[35] Cited in Philip Graham Ryken, *Discovering God: In Stories from the Bible* (Phillipsburg, NJ: P&R Publishing, 1999), 123.

[36] Ibid., 98.

[37] Isaac Watts, "Eternal Power, Whose High Abode," 1706.

[38] C. H. Spurgeon, cited in Stephen McCaskell, comp., *Through the Eyes of C. H. Spurgeon: Quotes from a Reformed Baptist Preacher* (Brenham, TX: Lucid Books, 2012), 98.

[39] *The Spurgeon Study Bible* (Nashville, TN: Holman Bible Publishers, 2017), 805.

[40] Andrew Murray, cited in Ray Pritchard, *Green Pastures, Quiet Waters: Refreshing Moments from the Psalms* (Chicago, IL: Moody Press, 1999), 59–60.

[41] Charles Haddon Spurgeon, cited in Tom Carter, comp., *Spurgeon At His Best* (Grand Rapids, MI: Baker Book House), 133.

[42] C. S. Lewis, cited in Dan DeWitt, *Christ or Chaos* (Wheaton, IL: Crossway, 2016), 83.

[43] Isaac Watts, "I Sing the Mighty Power of God," 1715.

[44] A. W. Tozer, *Meditations on the Trinity* (Chicago, IL: Moody Publishers, n.d.), 37–38.

[45] Gregg Allison, *The Baker Compact Dictionary of Theological Terms* (Grand Rapids, MI: Baker Books, 2016), 151–152.

Chapter 4: Pondering the Imponderable (2)

[1] Gregg Allison, *The Baker Compact Dictionary of Theological Terms* (Grand Rapids, MI: Baker Books, 2016), 100–101.

[2] Reginald Heber, "Holy, Holy, Holy," 1826.

[3] Donald S. Whitney, *Praying the Bible* (Wheaton, IL: Crossway, 2015), 13.

[4] Elisabeth Elliot, *The Music of His Promises: Listening to God with Love, Trust, and Obedience* (Ann Arbor, MI: Servant Publications, 2000), 117.

[5] Allan Bloom, cited in Randy Alcorn, *The Grace and Truth Paradox* (Sisters, OR: Multnomah Publishers, 2003), 56.

[6] Paul Enns, *The Moody Handbook of Theology*, revised and expanded (Chicago, IL: Moody Publishers, 2014), 198.

[7] William Walsham How, "O Word of God Incarnate," 1867.

[8] Adrian P. Rogers, *Adrianisms: The Wit and Wisdom of Adrian Rogers* (Memphis, TN: Love Worth Finding Ministries, 2006), 128.

[9] Martin Luther, "A Mighty Fortress Is Our God," 1529.

10 Cited in D. A. Carson, *For the Love of God: A Daily Companion for Discovering the Riches of God's Word, Vol. 2* (Wheaton, IL: Crossway Books, 1999), May 27 reading.

11 James R Lowell (1819–1891), adapted by Richard T. Bewes, C. Richard Bewes/Jubilate Hymns Ltd. copyrightmanager@jubilatehymns.co.uk used by permission.

12 Charles Wesley, "And Can It Be?" 1738.

13 These verses are usually quoted without attribution.

14 John MacArthur, *The MacArthur New Testament Commentary* (Nashville, TN: Thomas Nelson Publishers, 2007), 442.

15 John Owen, cited in Tim Chester, *Into His Presence: Praying with the Puritans* (Great Britain: The Good Book Company, 2022), 12.

16 Charles Wesley, "Love Divine, All Loves Excelling," 1747.

17 Francis Scott Key, "Lord, with Glowing Heart I'd Praise Thee," 1814.

18 Ron Prosise, *Preaching Illustrations from Church History* (The Woodlands, TX: Kress Biblical Resources, 2016), 6.

19 Charles Hodge, *A Commentary on Ephesians* (Carlisle, PA: Banner of Truth, 1964), 17.

20 Matthew Henry, cited in *Church History Study Bible: Voices from the Past, Wisdom for the Present* (Wheaton, IL: Crossway, 2023), 5

21 William Cowper, cited in Faith Cook, *Our Hymn-Writers and Their Hymns* (Carlisle, PA: Evangelical Press, 2005), 221.

22 David Dickson, cited in Peter Jeffery, *Believers Need the Gospel: Reaffirming the Gospel Message for Today's Christians* (Amityville, NY: Calvary Press, 2000), 22.

23 Annie Johnson Flint, "He Giveth More Grace," circa 1922 (lyrics).

24 Jerry Bridges cited in Tim Challies, *Words from the Wise: Knowing and Enjoying God* (Eugene, OR: Harvest House Publishers, 2021), 48.

25 John Bunyan, cited in *Complete Biblical Library: The Christian Classics Series, Volume 5: Morning and Evening, Charles H. Spurgeon, and Quotes Through the Centuries* (Springfield, MO: World Library Press Inc., 1999), 351.

26 Author unknown, sixth-century poem translated from Latin by Gabriel Gillett.

27 Steven J. Lawson, *Show Me Your Glory: Understanding the Majestic Splendor of God* (Orlando, FL: Reformation Trust, 2020), 145.

28 J. Gresham Machen, cited in Steven Lawson, *Show Me Your Glory: Understanding the Majestic Splendor of God* (Orlando, FL: Reformation Trust Publishing, 2020), 15.

29 George Herbert, "Teach Me, My God and King," 1633.

30 John Piper, *Astonished by God: Ten Truths to Turn the World Upside Down* (Minneapolis, MN: Published for Desiring God by Cruciform Press, 2018), 28.

31 Jerry Bridges, *The Joy of Fearing God* (Colorado Springs, CO: Waterbrook Press, 1997), 3.

32 JR Vassar, *Glory Hunger: God, the Gospel, and Our Quest for Something More* (Wheaton, IL: Crossway, 2015, 61.

33 Ibid., 79.

34 H. A. Cesar Malan, "Praise the Lord's Name," 1827.

35 A. B. Simpson, *The Mercy of God*, 1891.

36 David Clarkson, cited in Tim Chester, *Into His Presence: Praying with the Puritans* (Great Britain: The Good Book Company, 2022), 17.

37 Walter Chalmers Smith, "Immortal, Invisible, God Only Wise," 1867.

Chapter 5: Promises Too Good to Be True…If Made by Anyone but God!

1   Isaac Ambrose, cited in Robert Elmer, ed., *Piercing Heaven—Prayers of the Puritans* (Bellingham, WA, 2019), 24.

2   Corrie ten Boom, cited in Tim Challies, *Words from the Wise: Knowing and Enjoying God* (Eugene, OR: Harvest House Publishers, 2021), 84.

3   Charles R. Swindoll, *Second Wind: Fresh Hope for the Road Ahead* (Portland, OR: Multnomah Press, 1977).

4   Samuel Clark, cited in J. I. Packer, *Knowing God* (Downers Grove, IL: reprinted by InterVarsity Press, 2021, originally published, Hodder and Stoughton Limited, London, 1973), 115.

5   Brother Lawrence, *The Practice of the Presence of God* (Old Tappan, NJ: Fleming H. Revell Company, 1958), 45.

6   "Be thou my Vision," eighth-century Irish hymn; tr. Mary Elizabeth Byrne, 1905.

7   Augustus Toplady, "A Debtor to Mercy Alone," 1771.

8   Minnie Haskins, cited in Gordon J. Keddie, *Prayers of the Bible: 366 Devotionals to Encourage Your Prayer Life* (Pittsburgh, PA: Crown & Covenant Publications, 2017), 3.

9   John Rippon's Selection of Hymns, "How Firm a Foundation," 1878.

10 Thomas Brooks, cited in Wayne Stiles, *Going Places with God: A Devotional Journey Through the Lands of the Bible* (Ventura, CA: Regal Books from Gospel Light, 2006), 96.

11 Cited in Roy B. Zuck, *The Speaker's Quote Book* (Grand Rapids, MI: Kregel Publications, Academic and Professional, 1997, 2009), 425.

12 John Rippon's Selection of Hymns, "How Firm a Foundation," 1878.

13 Raymond C. Ortlund Jr., *Isaiah: God Saves Sinners* (Wheaton, IL: Crossway Books, 2005), 255.

14 Robert J. Morgan, *The Strength You Need: The Twelve Great Strength Passages of the Bible* (Nashville, TN: W Publishing Group, an imprint of Thomas Nelson, 2016), 12.

15 Caroline V. Sandell-Berg, "Day by Day," 1865.

16 Charles H. Spurgeon, cited in Robert J. Morgan, *The Promise: God Works All Things Together for Your Good* (Nashville, TN: B&H Publishing Group, 2010), xi.

17 Jonathan Edwards, cited in Mark Jones, *God Is: A Devotional Guide to the Attributes of God* (Wheaton, IL: Crossway, 2017), 12.

18 Louisa M. R. Stead, "'Tis So Sweet to Trust in Jesus." 1882.

19 Charles R. Swindoll, *Wisdom for the Way: Wise Words for Busy People* (Nashville, TN: Thomas Nelson, 2001), 25.

20 Elisabeth Elliot, *The Music of His Promises: Listening to God with Love, Trust, and Obedience* (Ann Arbor, MI: Servant Publications, 2000), 5.

21 Robert Lowry, "How Can I Keep from Singing?" 1901.

22 Savonarola, cited in Erwin Lutzer, *Christ Among Other gods: A Defense of Christ in an Age of Tolerance* (Chicago, IL: Moody Press, 1994), 160–161.

23 F. B. Meyer, *Daily Prayers* (Ross-shire, Great Britain: Christian Focus Publications, 2007), December 15 reading.

24 Cited in Warren W. Wiersbe, *Key Words of the Christian Life: Understanding and Applying Their Meanings* (Grand Rapids, MI: Baker Books, 2002), 105.

25 William Cowper, from "Holy Lord God, I Love Thy Truth," cited in *Church History Study Bible: Voices from the Past, Wisdom for the Present* (Wheaton, IL: Crossway, 2023), 1929.

26 Vance Havner, *The Best of Vance Havner* (Grand Rapids, MI: Baker Book House, 1980, Reprinted from Fleming H. Revell, 1969), 41.

27 Augustine, cited in Peter Jeffery, *Bitesize Theology* (Webster, NY: Evangelical Press, 2000), 97.

28 James M. Hamilton Jr., *What Is Biblical Theology? A Guide to the Bible's Story, Symbolism, and Patterns* (Wheaton, IL: Crossway, 2014), 114.

29 Randy Alcorn, *Money, Possessions, and Eternity*, rev. ed. (Wheaton, IL: Tyndale House Publishers, revised and updated edition, 2003), 38.

30 C. S. Lewis, *Mere Christianity* (New York: HarperCollins Publishers, 2001, originally published, C. S. Lewis Pte. Ltd., 1952), 136–137.

31 Richard Baxter, cited in Alistair Begg, *Pray Big: Learn to Pray Like an Apostle* (England, UK: The Good Book Company, 2019), 55.

32 This account told in Peter Jeffery, *Windows of Truth* (Carlisle, PA: The Banner of Truth Trust, 1992), 9.

33 Thomas Manton, cited in Joel R. Beeke, *A Faithful Church Member* (Carlisle, PA: EP Books, 2011), 41.

34 "Praise the Lord! Ye Heavens Adore Him," Words: Anonymous.

Chapter 6: Correctly Fearing God

1 Joel R. Beeke and Brian Cosby, *None Else: 31 Meditations on God's Character and Attributes* (Grand Rapids, MI: Reformation Heritage Books, 2020), 8.

2   John Stott, *Authentic Christianity*, From the Writings of John Stott: Chosen and introduced by Timothy Dudley-Smith (Downers Grove, IL: InterVarsity Press, 1995), 17.

3   Brother Lawrence, cited in Patrick Kavanaugh, *Worship—A Way of Life* (Grand Rapids, MI: Chosen Books, 2001), 195.

4   T. S. Eliot, cited in Michael Horton, *We Believe: Recovering the Essentials of the Apostles' Creed* (Nashville, TN: Word Publishing, 1998), 3.

5   John Piper, *Don't Waste Your Life: Group Study Edition* (Wheaton, IL: Crossway, 2007, text updated 2009), 33.

6   John D. Hannah, *Our Legacy: The History of Christian Doctrine* (Colorado Springs, CO: NavPress, 2001), 11.

7   Ibid.

8   Charles Ryrie, *Ryrie's Practical Guide to Communicating Bible Doctrine* (Nashville, TN: Broadman and Holman Publishers, 2005), 19.

9   Michael Reeves, *Rejoice and Tremble: The Surprising Good News of the Fear of the Lord* (Wheaton, IL: Crossway, 2021), 43.

10 D. Stuart Briscoe, *Vital Truths to Shape Your Life* (Wheaton, IL: Tyndale House Publishers, 2002), 56.

11 Kelly M. Kapic, *A Little Book for New Theologians: Why and How to Study Theology* (Downers Grove, IL: IVP Academic, an imprint of InterVarsity Press, 2012), 27.

12 Henry Blackaby, *Experiencing the Word New Testament* (Nashville, TN: Holman Bible Publishers, 2008), 341.

13 Aiden Wilson Tozer, *The Quotable Tozer: A Topical Compilation of the Wisdom and Insight of A. W. Tozer*, James L. Snyder, Compiler and Editor (Minneapolis, MN: Bethany House Publishers, 2018), 152.

14 Steven J. Lawson, *Holman Old Testament Commentary, Psalms 1–75* (Nashville, TN: Broadman and Holman Publishers, Holman Bible Reference, 2003), 143.

15 Marvin Hamlisch, cited in D. Stuart Briscoe, *Vital Truths to Shape Your Life* (Wheaton, IL: Tyndale House Publishers, 2002), 58.

16 Frederick Nolan, cited in Steven J. Lawson, *Holman Old Testament Commentary, Psalms 1–75* (Nashville, TN: Broadman and Holman Publishers, Holman Bible Reference, 2003), 142.

17 "At All Times I Will Bless the Lord," in *The Book of Psalms for Worship* (Pittsburgh, PA: Crown & Covenant Publications, 2010), 34.

18 Daniel Webster in Kenneth D. Boa and Robert M. Bowman Jr., *20 Compelling Evidences That God Exists: Discover Why Believing in God Makes So Much Sense* (Tulsa, OK: RiverOak Publishing, 2002), 182.

19 This story told by Roy J. Fish, *Giving a Good Invitation* (Nashville, TN: Broadman Press, 1974), 36–37.

Chapter 7: Correctly Bearing God's Image

1 John Stonestreet, Introduction in Glenn Sunshine and Timothy Padgett, *The Image Restored: The Imago Dei and Creation* (Colorado Springs, CO: Colson Press, 2021), 7.

2 Wayne Grudem, *Systematic Theology: An Introduction to Biblical Doctrine,* Second Edition (Grand Rapids, MI: Zondervan Academic, 1994, 2020), 568.

3 Warren W. Wiersbe, *Key Words of the Christian Life: Understanding and Applying Their Meanings* (Grand Rapids, MI: Baker Book House Company, 2002), 107.

4 F. B. Meyer, *Daily Prayers* (Ross-shire, Great Britain: Christian Focus Publications, 2007), July 31 reading.

5 C. S. Lewis, *Mere Christianity* (New York: reprinted by HarperCollins Publishers, 2001, originally published 1952, C. S. Lewis Pte. Ltd.), 49.

6 Robert Charles Sproul, *In the Presence of God* (Nashville, TN: Word Publishing, 1999), 200.

7 G. K. Chesterton, cited in Trevin Wax, *This Is Our Time: Everyday Myths in Light of the Gospel* (Nashville: B&H Publishing Group, 2017), 190.

8 Horatius Bonar, cited in Erwin W. Lutzer, *No Reason to Hide: Standing for Christ in a Collapsing Culture* (Eugene, OR: Harvest House Publishers, 2022), 168.

9 Vance Havner, *The Vance Havner Notebook*, compiled by Dennis J. Hester (Grand Rapids, MI: Baker Book House, 1989), 155–156.

10 Randy Alcorn, with Stephanie Anderson, *Pro-Choice or Pro-Life: Examining 15 Pro-Choice Claims—What Do Facts & Common Sense Tell Us?* (Sandy, OR: Eternal Perspective Ministries, 2020), 114.

11 Gordon J. Keddie, *Prayers of the Bible: 366 Devotionals to Encourage Your Prayer Life* (Pittsburgh, PA: Crown & Covenant Publications, 2017), 4.

12 Ingrid Newkirk, cited in Richard E. Simmons III, *Reflections on the Existence of God: A Series of Essays* (Birmingham, AL: Union Hill Publishing, 2019), 28.

13 Ingrid Newkirk, cited in John MacArthur, General Editor, *Think Biblically! Recovering a Christian Worldview* (Wheaton, IL: Crossway Books, 2003), 73.

14 Richard E. Simmons III, *Reflections on the Existence of God*, 29.

15 John MacArthur, *Think Biblically!*, 73.

16 Ibid., 74.

17 Richard E. Simmons III, *Reflections on the Existence of God*, 29.

18 C. S. Lewis, cited in Scott Larsen, General Ed., *Indelible Ink: 22 Prominent Christian Leaders Discuss the Books That Shape Their Faith* (Colorado Springs, CO: Waterbrook Press, 2003), 92.

19 John Stott, *Authentic Christianity*, from the writings of John Stott: chosen and introduced by Timothy Dudley-Smith (Downers Grove, IL: InterVarsity Press, 1995), 139.

20 Glen Scrivener, *Reading Between the Lines: Old Testament Daily Readings, Vol. 1* (Leyland, England: 10 Publishing, 2018), 26–27.

[21] Joseph Hart, "Come, Ye Sinners, Poor and Needy," 1759.

[22] D. M. Lloyd-Jones, *Knowing the Times: Addresses Delivered on Various Occasions, 1942–1977* (Carlisle, PA: The Banner of Truth Trust, first published 1989, reprinted 2013), 292.

[23] John MacArthur, *The MacArthur Study Bible* (Wheaton, IL: Crossway, 2010), 1872.

[24] Louie Giglio, *Waiting Here for You: An Advent Journey of Hope* (Nashville, TN: Thomas Nelson, 2015), 26.

[25] Herman Ridderbos, cited in Ligon Duncan, *Fear Not! Death and the Afterlife from a Christian Perspective* (Ross-shire, Great Britain: Christian Focus Publications, 2008), 41.

[26] Charles Wesley, "And Can It Be?" 1738.

[27] Augustine, cited in Charles Colson, *God and Government: An Insider's View on the Boundaries Between Faith and Politics* (Grand Rapids MI: Zondervan, 2007), 391.

[28] Matthew Bridges, "Crown Him with Many Crowns," 1851.

[29] G. Campbell Morgan, cited in Paul Enns, *Approaching God: Daily Readings in Systematic Theology* (Chicago, IL: Moody Press, 1991), December 1 reading.

[30] Os Guinness, *Carpe Diem Redeemed: Seizing the Day, Discerning the Times* (Downers Grove, IL: InterVarsity Press, 2019), 18.

[31] Henri Cesar Malan, "It is Not Death to Die," 1841.

[32] Isaac Watts, cited in Faith Cook, *Our Hymn-Writers and Their Hymns* (Carlisle, PA: Evangelical Press, 2005), 50.

[33] J. I. Packer, *Concise Theology: A Guide to Historic Christian Beliefs* (Wheaton, IL: Tyndale House Publishers, 1993), 267.

[34] William Jenkyn, cited in Joel R. Beeke, *Overcoming the World: Grace to Win the Daily Battle* (Phillipsburg, NJ: P&R Publishing, 2005), 32.

[35] Gordon J. Keddie, *Prayers of the Bible: 366 Devotionals to Encourage Your Prayer Life* (Pittsburgh, PA: Crown & Covenant Publications, 2017), 17.

[36] Johann Mentzer, "O That I Had a Thousand Voices," 1704.

Conclusion: Thinking Rightly…Living Boldly…Trusting Fully…

[1] John Adams, cited in James Emery White, *Serious Times: Making Your Life Matter in an Urgent Day* (Downers Grove, IL: InterVarsity Press, 2004), 9.

[2] Roy Aldrich cited in Charles R. Swindoll, *Growing Deep in the Christian Life: Returning to Our Roots* (Portland, OR: Multnomah Press, 1986), 65–66.

[3] James Emory White, *The Church in an Age of Crisis: 25 New Realities Facing Christianity* (Grand Rapids: Baker Books, 2012), 10.

[4] Mark A. Noll, *The Scandal of the Evangelical Mind* (Grand Rapids: Eerdmans, 1994), 3.

[5] C. H. Spurgeon, cited in J. I. Packer, *Growing in Christ* (Wheaton, IL: Crossway Books, 1994), xiii.

[6] Jonathan Edwards, cited in Tim Dowley, ed., *Introduction to the History of Christianity* (Minneapolis, MN: Fortress Press, 1995, first published by Lion Publishing, 1977), 440.

[7] David Platt, foreword in John Piper, *Risk is Right* (Wheaton, IL: Crossway, 2013), 8–9.

[8] William Williams, cited in Peter Jeffery, *Windows of Truth* (Carlisle, PA: The Banner of Truth Trust, 1992), 42.

[9] Martin Luther, "A Mighty Fortress Is Our God," 1529.

[10] Aleksandr Solzhenitsyn cited in David Aikman, *Great Souls: Six Who Changed the Century* (Nashville, TN: Word Publishing, 1998), 182.

[11] John Newton, "Rejoice, Believer, in the Lord," 1779.

[12] Calvin Miller, *Letters to a Young Pastor* (Colorado Springs, CO: David C Cook, 2011), dedication page.

[13] This account told in Ron Prosise, *Preaching Illustrations from Church History* (The Woodlands, TX: Kress Biblical Resources, 2016), 197, 198.

[14] C. S. Lewis, *The Weight of Glory: And Other Addresses* (New York: reprinted by HarperCollins Publishers, 2001, originally published, C. S. Lewis Pte. Ltd., 1949), 46.

[15] John Guest, cited in Scott Larsen, General Ed., *Indelible Ink: 22 Prominent Christian Leaders Discuss the Books That Shape Their Faith* (Colorado Springs, CO: Waterbrook Press, 2003), 248.

[16] John Oxenham, cited in V. Raymond Edman, *The Disciplines of Life* (Minneapolis, MN: World Wide Publications, 1972, Scripture Press Foundation, 1948), 202.

[17] Jean Sophia Pigott, "Jesus, I Am Resting, Resting," 1876.

[18] Frances R. Havergal, "Like a River Glorious," 1874.

Appendix 2: Building Your Life upon the Gospel

[1] Trevin Wax, cited in Randy Alcorn, *It's All About Jesus: A Treasury of Insights on Our Savior, Lord, and Friend* (Eugene, OR: Harvest House Publishers, 2020), 275.

[2] C. J. Mahaney, *Living the Cross Centered Life* (Sisters, OR: Multnomah Publishers, 2006), 132.

[3] John R. W. Stott, *Authentic Christianity*, From the Writings of John Stott: Chosen and introduced by Timothy Dudley-Smith (Downers Grove, IL: InterVarsity Press, 1995), 166.

[4] Martin H. Manser, Alister E. McGrath, J. I. Packer, Donald J. Wiseman, *Zondervan Dictionary of Bible Themes: The Accessible and Comprehensive Tool for Topical Studies* (Grand Rapids, MI: Zondervan Publishing House, 1999), 558.

[5] Timothy Keller, cited in Tim Challies, *Words from the Wise: Knowing and Enjoying God* (Eugene, OR: Harvest House Publishers, 2021), 218.

[6] Philip P. Bliss, "Hallelujah, what a Savior!" 1875.

ABOUT THE AUTHOR

Marc Drake, a native of Georgia, is a graduate of Southwestern Baptist Theological Seminary (MDiv) and Luther Rice Seminary (DMin). He is also a fellow with the Stephen Olford Center for Biblical Preaching and a fellow with the Colson Center for Christian Worldview. Marc has pastored churches in four states over a period of forty-five years, as well as having preached and ministered in several other countries. Marc and his wife, Pamela, live in New Braunfels, Texas, where they enjoy time with their children and grandchildren, fellowship and serve with their church family, and delight in the history and scenery of the Texas Hill Country.

Printed in the USA
CPSIA information can be obtained
at www.ICGtesting.com
LVHW041049241124
797242LV00001B/107

* 9 7 9 8 8 9 3 0 9 2 7 7 6 *